Brummie Anglers
The Early Adventures of Two Fishing Friends

Written and illustrated by
John Anscombe

With foreword by
Mick Brown

This book is dedicated with heartfelt gratitude:

To my wonderful parents, whose love for fishing sparked my passion, and to my dear late brother Bob, whose endless chauffeuring and shared journeys with Mick and me hold a special place in my heart.

To Mick's incredible family, whose warmth and hospitality made me feel like one of their own, enhancing our fishing escapades with laughter and camaraderie.

To my beloved wife Carol and our children Andrea and Philip, whose support and encouragement have motivated me to share my fishing tales.

And to Mick Brown, my steadfast friend and fishing companion, whose companionship and shared passion have filled my life with joy and adventure.

CONTENTS

Dedication
Foreword
Preface
About The Author   87

Foreword

If I had to look back to an era of my fondest angling memories, it would surely be those ten formative years spent with my lifetime best mate Johnny Anscombe when we were both young, fit, adventurous, and full of ideas and plans. Words struggle to adequately describe how much those fishing days spent together mean to me.

Time has moved on and taken us through life's ups and downs until we have reached a ripe old age where we can put meaning into our experiences. Without any doubt in my mind, the years that John describes in this book bring back to life a gentler age of angling where friendship and fun triumphed over egos and commercialism.

For me, this book records precious memories from which more mature readers might draw their own. In a world that has changed so dramatically in the following years, I hope that younger readers will appreciate from Johns's stories that the journey is just as important as the result.

We are still those same Brummie lads of yesteryear, still talking about the sport we love, even if we are not practicing it as much!

Mick Brown

Preface

I found writing this memoir difficult, repeatedly having to refer back to events via worn-out notebooks and diaries, old photos, text messages and phone calls. At last, it's finished and ready to be presented. I can now only sit back and hope you find it enjoyable.

The following chapters are largely about fishing with my best pal, the gently ageing, highly experienced and expert predator angler, Mick Brown.

I also hope readers will discover more than that, as I share with you some of the many incidents and adventures that have peppered our friendship over the last sixty years. We have both participated in and been obsessed with angling since we were youngsters in short trousers to senior citizens in winter thermals.

It is true to say that, excluding the normal growing-up activities with our families, schools and jobs, fishing of any kind has filled most of our spare time.

It is also true to say that we will continue, only ceasing when the inevitable passing of time or illness stops us from holding a rod and line over a body of water, eagerly awaiting the next bite or pull of the rod tip. Mick recently told me that with the arthritis in his hand getting worse, he is doubting if he will be able to pike fish this winter. However, I just know he will find a way to carry on fishing and I won't be surprised if more very big pikes end up in his landing net. It would be foolish of me not to anticipate a message from him, telling me about yet another recently caught 30-pounder.

John Anscombe

Throughout our lives, we will meet thousands of different people from a multitude of different backgrounds, ages and religions. Some just become casual acquaintances and fall by the wayside or drift out of our lives, due to unforeseen circumstances. Occasionally we will meet a person and a friendship develops, and if you are very lucky, it could become a special relationship lasting many decades. This was and still is the situation between Mick Brown and me. He will always be my best friend, second only to my lovely wife Carol.

I have known Mick for sixty years, and throughout that time, we have always managed to keep in contact. Even when I got married to Carol in 1973 and moved to New Zealand on a five-year work contract. With half the globe standing between us, we still kept in touch by communicating through Christmas cards containing handwritten notes about all sorts of topics, but mainly about the recent fish we'd caught. If we had a lot to say we'd use the blue airmail letters. Telephone calls in 1973 at £1 a minute were for emergencies only! My fishing conversations would have been so much easier had the internet been available.

The notion of writing a few chapters about our fishing history and friendship came together by pure accident. A few seasons ago whilst we were piking on the River Nene near Northampton, we were reliving some of the many fishing adventures we had shared. We both agreed that instead of just talking about past events it could potentially make an interesting read.

As a result, I finally decided to put pen to paper. It's a daunting task, taking me almost a year to write anything of consequence!

Mick and I encountered each other when we both began our first proper employment after leaving school in the summer of 1963. We were both accepted as engineering apprentices at Joseph Lucas Ltd. in Birmingham. We became nodding acquaintances whilst waiting in line to punch in at the clocking-in machine situated by the wooden entrance gate to the workshops. Initially, I was a little wary of Mick. He sported thick black hair swept back in a ducktail style, and with his pointed black shoes and drainpipe trousers, he was not typical of my other local friends. However, there was a dress code during our apprenticeship comprising green overalls and toe protector shoes, usually brown, which meant we more or less looked the same. This was insisted on by the staff to help break down barriers as we were learning our engineering skills.

The Lucas Engineering School was, at the time, one of the most recognised training schemes in the country. As well as receiving a certified five years of engineering training it also provided technical courses at various colleges. Personnel development was also encouraged, providing many different sporting activities including football, rugby, judo, weight training, fencing and "Yes!", a fishing club!

We both individually joined the club and then kept bumping into each other at the weigh-ins after the various contests. As we talked and got to know each other it became apparent that our young lives had many things in common. Our friendship continued to strengthen and at lunch, we joined up with a bunch of other apprentices in the works canteen over a game of Last Card.

Mick and I would discuss our upbringings and share jokes and lads' stories from our childhoods. It transpired we were both Brummies and living with our parents, me from Winson Green and Mick from Acocks Green. Both of our families were crazy about fishing, Mick's dad Ralph and my dad George were good local anglers who fished most weekends and won several club matches, often finishing in the prizes after the weigh-ins. Both our extended families also fished, including our brothers, Mick's uncle Arthur and my uncle Harry.

We had both started fishing around six years old, joining our dads, around the Midland's rivers and canals. We tagged along to the weekend matches and fished for as long as possible after the match was over.

We quickly found out that in our last couple of years at senior school we'd shared the same hardships, resisting and defending ourselves against aggressive bullying from other pupils and teachers. We dished out retribution when necessary and had to then accept the penalties for our actions. It seemed we were both getting prepared for the ups and downs that life would throw at us when we finally left school.

The similarities were uncanny, it was as if destiny had thrown us together to become long-time fishing friends.

Whenever there was a Lucas' fishing match we would attend. Come wind, rain, sleet, or snow we would be there crouched over our creels, intently watching our floats. I remember one match in particular. We were fishing the River Trent on a bitter, rainy day and I was in a terrible pitch. The river was thundering past and I only had a tiny little slack, in which I ledgered bread flake. I only had one bite in four hours, but it did produce a very nice roach of 13oz. It gave me third place and a prize of a box of assorted biscuits. The unluckiest angler on that day was a rugby friend called Matt Dewsbury. He was really chuffed with catching a 1lb 14oz trout and was jumping with joy at the weigh-in until he was told that his trout could not be counted as it was out of season.

A few months into our apprenticeships Mick and I decided that just going to weekend matches was not going to satisfy our growing appetites. The big problem was where to fish after work. We needed somewhere local and **easy to get to.**

The answer was a lake near Mick's home in Fox Hollies Park. Well, I say lake, but it was more of a large pond. It was a typical park, mixed species fishery. From then onwards, at least once a week after work, we would catch the train together back to Mick's house. After a meal of egg and chips, provided by his lovely mum, we would take the short walk down to the park, armed with a float rod, a few items of tackle and whatever bait was left from the previous weekend. This was normally a few maggots, some worms, and a few slices of bread. We would quietly fish, taking turns to catch roach and small bream.

Towards evening the reeds close to us would start twitching and swaying from side to side. Mick put this down to the elusive tench that lived in the lake. Every season the odd one would get caught, but more by accident than design. It became apparent that Mick was determined to catch one of these shy tench. So, after I had finished up to catch the last bus across town to my house, Mick fished on. As it got dark he would sneak away to hide in the nearby bushes. There with his rod, landing net, and tackle box also hidden, he would crouch down out of sight and wait for the park keeper to finish his patrol around the lake. Fishing after dark was not allowed, so the last duty of the park keeper was to ensure that all anglers had gone home. The keeper would eventually leave the park and Mick would strain his ears to catch the sound of the squeaking gates and click of the lock. He would then leave his hiding place and carry on fishing. And it wasn't long before he started to outwit the crafty tench!

These fish had learnt that after dark lots of odds and ends of bait would be disposed of in the margins. By working their way around the reed beds they'd confidently mop up anything in their path. I can imagine Mick's float gently swaying before sliding away and disappearing into the reeds, followed by the hefty thump of a well-hooked tench.

These sessions, on occasion, were not without incident. Sometimes, drunken youths would cut through the park and relieve themselves near the water, which could have proved embarrassingly difficult for Mick. Courting couples would also take advantage of the park bushes and lush grass, especially during the summer's long evenings. I am sure Mick, being a gentleman, kept his eyes firmly on his float.

Another incident involved a stray dog. One evening, as darkness fell, Mick had crouched down and was about to cast a piece of neatly hooked bread flake into the margins, when out of the bushes appeared a dog. Very hungry it grabbed the bread flake in its mouth, and in fright it took off around the towpath, the hook beginining to dig into the dog's mouth.

Not knowing whether to take to the bushes or stay on the path the dog completed a full lap of the lake with Mick chasing after it, rod held high, winding like mad trying to regain line. Finally, Mick got close enough to grab the dog's neck and the poor animal gave up struggling. Luckily the hook just dropped out of the dog's mouth.

When Mick was night fishing at Fox Hollies Park he found it difficult to use a standard circular-handled torch to illuminate his float as they tended to roll around on the sloping bankside, especially when windy. He found a solution by using the lamp from his bicycle. It had a square battery box and wide beam and remained stable under most conditions. It was one of the first of our many fishing improvisations.

Reaching seventeen we started meeting for lunch with other apprentice friends at the Lord Clifton, a local pub still there to this day. After drinking shandy, playing darts and eating crusty ham rolls Mick and I would talk about our last weekend's fishing with our Dads. These were detailed blow-by-blow accounts about various fish we had caught from the Rivers Severn, Trent or Avon in Warwickshire. They were exciting conversations for us, but they bored the pants off our friends. Often the term, "Here we go again," could be heard from the bottom of a half-pint glass.

Travelling west to fish the mighty River Wye in Shropshire, Mick's dad Ralph would invite me to join them to fish the Birmingham Anglers Association (BAA) Waters at Symonds Yat, Herefordshire. Mick and I would mainly fish the faster stretches, especially the rapids, and catch chub after chub on bread flake which we fished under a large, heavily shotted homemade float. Ralph meanwhile would fish for the salmon, and I still have a photo of Mick holding a 22lb fresh run salmon caught by his dad.

Ralph and Mick's uncle Arthur were never ones to miss an opportunity and with the aid of fishing contacts, they gained access to another short River Wye salmon beat not on the BAA waters. It was by pure accident that they got to fish it. They were travelling back to Birmingham in Arthur's Morris Traveller after a day's fishing on the Wye when they spotted an old lady struggling to carry a heavy load of shopping. They pulled over and offered to give her a lift home, which turned out to be a little cottage, and she invited them in for afternoon tea as a thank-you for their kindness. She asked them where they had been, and after being told they had been fishing the river Wye she stated that coincidentally the Wye ran right past the end of her back garden. She asked if they would like to have a look and I can imagine both

Ralph and Arthur leaping out of their chairs with excitement. She then proceeded to show them not only the river but also the Salmon Beat and a small rowing boat. After another cup of tea, and no doubt a piece of homemade cake, she stated that it was a joy to have company and any time they were passing to call in for a cuppa. Then she adds, "Oh and by the way I have the fishing rights to the river stretch behind my back garden, and you can fish it any time you wish."

It wasn't anything special, yielding the very occasional salmon, but the bonus was their access to that rowing boat. They also knew that just at the end of their stretch, and at the start of the next downstream "Private Members Only" stretch, there was a much more productive salmon-holding area. So, they would anchor the boat directly at the end of their run, and trot down a prawn or bunch of worms into the members-only salmon pool. Their catch rate improved considerably, but they could only get away with fishing like that when there were no private members on the bank. As you can imagine the members would complain bitterly and argue that Ralph and Arther were fishing illegally. But were they? I don't know, but I do know they caught some quality salmon. They took advantage of the circumstances presented to them and reaped the benefits.

One day, out of the blue, Mick said that his family were going camping and fishing for a week on the River Ithon near Llandrindod Wells, Central Wales. He asked if I would like to join them. Would I ever! I had previously fished the Ithon when I was around ten. I remember standing in the chilly water on a summer's day, trotting a fat worm down the current, catching trout after trout using a ten-foot bamboo rod and wooden centre pin reel.

Arranging to pick me up from the opposite side of Birmingham caused logistical problems as our only form of transport was Ralph's old green Bedford Van complete with sliding side doors. It was always parked overnight at Mick's house in Acocks Green, and, if I wanted to go, it was up to me to get over to his house. This meant taking the seven-mile trip by bus, fully loaded down with fishing tackle and a backpack of clothing.

So very early on the morning of our trip, I think it was a Saturday, I caught the number 96 bus into the city centre, where I could disembark and catch any of three buses to Acocks Green, finishing with a four hundred meter walk to Mick's house.

The 96 bus was almost empty as I boarded, the Bull Ring shoppers were not yet up and about. All the buses at this time had a conductor as well as a driver, and the conductors were not to be messed with! Most were friendly, but some were so full of themselves that if you gave them the slightest excuse they would kick you off the bus. After getting on the number 96 I sat on a double seat close to the stairs, waiting to pay for my ticket, the right money clenched in my fist. My creel and backpack were on the seat beside me, and the rod bag was balanced between my legs. I sat peering out of the fogged-up windows, eager and excited.

The conductor was one of the short-tempered types. Immediately upon giving me my ticket he told me that all my tackle would have to be moved from the seats and put under the stairway that was reserved for pushchairs and prams. When I mentioned I hadn't put it in there because it wasn't a pushchair or a pram his reply was to move the tackle or get off the bus. So, I moved it and sat back down in my seat, hoping the shaking of the bus would not dislodge my rod bag. Halfway to the city centre's terminal, a young mother boarded the bus with, you guessed it, a baby and a fold-up pushchair. The next few minutes were hectic! Trying to stay balanced on the rolling bus, I pulled out my backpack to make room for the pushchair. Unfortunately, it snagged on my rod bag and dragged it into the gangway. The conductor started to get angry, telling me to shift my gear or get off the bus as I was causing an obstruction. I politely pointed out to him that this was why I had kept my gear on the spare seat next to me in the first place, to avoid what just happened. My comment did not go down well as I was now embarrassing him. We continued to argue until we reached the terminal, where he was determined to have the last word, shouting as I disembarked, "And I don't want to see you on my bus again!" I felt like saying something like "Get a life you ignorant, aggressive f****r!" If I had the courage of Bill Bryson, maybe I would have.

With his words still ringing in my ears, I caught my second bus and crossed my fingers for a quiet onward journey to Mick's. The conductor on this bus turned out to be from Swansea. He was far more friendly as he was interested in my holiday on the River Ithon.

Eventually, I arrived at Mick's house, eager to start our adventure. I could see the loading of the Bedford van was in full swing. A human chain passed items from the front door into the van via the sliding doors. This strangely included their old settee from the lounge. You see the van only had a front bench seat which was already reserved for Ralph, Mick's mum Sylvia, and his sister Chris. In the back, the settee, now securely strapped in place, was for Mick's two younger brothers. The remaining floor area housed all the food and equipment. There was just enough room for Mick and I to squeeze in via the back doors. With only a couple of coats to sit on, we settled our bums down onto the plywood flooring, the loaded-down van springs compressed to their limits. We left Birmingham heading west on our ninety-mile journey to Wales.

On the way, Ralph suggested we stop for lunch at a quiet little pull-in they knew from previous trips close to Leominster. So we turned off the main road after travelling for a couple of hours. The pull-in turned out to be a layby right next to a small gravelled-bottomed, clear-flowing river.

Quick as a wink, Ralph was out of the driving seat and unloading his fishing creel, bait tin and ready-assembled twelve-foot match rod. I watched dumbfounded as he disappeared through the bushes. He set up his creel on the riverbank, threw in a handful of maggots and started to fish. Meanwhile Mick, his mum and his sister had unloaded camping chairs and a picnic table and were laying out drinks and sandwiches for everyone.

I looked at Mick and asked, "Is this a normal event?"

"Oh yes," said Mick in a matter-of-fact sort of way, "I expect we will be here for an hour or maybe longer."

So, we sat on the deck chairs drinking tea, eating sandwiches, and watching Ralph fish the River Arrow. He caught trout and grayling, and we cheered every time a fish slid over the landing net.

After what was more like two hours than one, we packed everything back into the van, and completed the journey to the Ithon, arriving mid-afternoon at the farm where we were going to camp for the week. The early summer weather was warm and embracing, and our evening meal of fried trout, peas, and tomato sauce was delicious. After finishing setting up our tents and sleeping quarters we retired to bed, already anticipating the arrival of a new day, and the opportunity to explore the river which steadily flowed through the meadows.

Finishing breakfast and the completion of our camping duties, Mick and I decided to walk the length of the stretch, and what a wonderful first encounter it was. It consisted of three sets of rapids, and below each one was a deep holding pool. Who knew what was lurking in their depths? Big chub, trout, sea trout, eels? We formulated a plan to fish the deeper pools during the early mornings and evenings. The rest of the days, in between meals and playing football with Mick's siblings, we would wander down the rest of the stretch and fish any likely-looking pitches as we encountered them.

We had already identified several big chub tucked under the opposite bank and hiding beneath the overhanging willows. Very quickly we found that the best way to catch these wonderfully clean, glistening chub was to select a shady spot and free-line a large piece of fluffy bread down the current. Because the clarity of the water was so good, it was possible to watch the white bread drift down and then see it get intercepted by a big white-mouthed chub. Sometimes they were gentle, but most times they grabbed it in a flash, viciously and greedily.

We lost count of the number of chub we caught over the first two days, but it was well over thirty. It became too easy.

On the third day, we changed over to fly fishing, continuing to catch chub but also catching the occasional grayling and trout. We had not yet learnt the art of dry fly fishing but we persevered using several homemade dry flies, including Iron Blues, March Browns, Hares Ears, Zulus, Blue Bottles and May Flys. After a day of constant casting we flopped down onto the bank to watch Ralph steadily, and with what seemed like little effort, catch trout and grayling until sunset.

Mick decided to finish off the day fishing in one of the pools below the rapids with a bunch of worms. Well into the evening Mick had a clunking bite. He hooked but unfortunately lost what we think was a salmon. Now it was my turn, and it wasn't long before the rod tip plunged around again. Yes, I was in! But this was no salmon, it was an eel, about 2lb. This was to be my biggest eel for some years.

The fourth day of our holiday provided us with different fishing opportunities. Ralph decided he was going to fish Llandrindod Boat Lake for crucian carp, and as we were finding catching the chub too easy, we went with him. Mick and I caught crucians and roach throughout the day, and not long before we were due to pack up his dad shouted for assistance. Ralph was playing a carp caught on bread flake. Mick helped land the fish. It was a 10lb mirror carp and the biggest fish we had ever seen. I had only ever caught one carp previously, on Sutton Park Boating Lake. I was eleven years old and it weighed 5lb. I had caught it with floating crust.

That day at Llandrindod was one Mick and I will always remember as it was our introduction to the boating lake, a site we would return to and fish extensively for carp throughout the early '70s.

There was something else besides the fishing that caught my eye whilst on this holiday, the farmer's daughter. Most days I would see her pass by driving the tractor, long black hair flowing in the breeze. She would smile and say hello, but I never seemed able to introduce myself properly. Time was running out. I found out she had a weekend job at a shoe shop in Llandrindod.

So, on the last Saturday of our holiday, I put aside my rod and caught the bus into town. I entered her shop on the pretext I needed a new pair of shoes for dancing at the Birmingham clubs. I explained that a pair of winklepickers, size 8, would be ideal. She promptly disappeared into the storeroom and returned with a black leather pair. Unfortunately, they had a rather unnecessary gold imitation plastic coat of arms attached to the side of each shoe.

But I was a sucker for a good-looking young lady, and, like an idiot I bought them on the understanding that she would meet me that evening at the side of the farmhouse. We met, held hands and kissed, and then much to my surprise she said goodnight and left me standing in the darkness. I saw her twice again before we left the campsite, but she was on the tractor and too busy to stop for a chat let alone anything else. I came to hate those shoes, they reminded me of how stupid I had been. Plus they were too narrow and left me with blisters every time I went dancing, especially whilst doing the twist. And those gold coats of arms I pulled off with a pair of pliers, leaving two small holes in each shoe. Not before time those shoes ended their life in the bin.

Before too long Mick's family invited me on a second week of camping and fishing, this time on the River Avon at Breamore, Hampshire. The private stretch of the river belonged to Ralph's commanding officer from his wartime army days. Once again the old green Bedford van was loaded to the roof, including the old settee. This time though there was no room for Mick and me to sit on the van's plywood floor.

To overcome this problem Ralph had pre-arranged train tickets for the two of us, from Acocks Green station into Birmingham Snow Hill and then south to Fordingbridge, Hampshire. Here we would be picked up by Ralph and the rest of the Brown family.

The journey was estimated at five hours, and Mick and I agreed it wouldn't be too much of a hassle. But what we didn't know until we were about to set off was that we'd have to take our fishing tackle with us. The back doors of the van were already beginning to bulge and a hefty shoulder was needed to lock the handle closed. There was no room in the van for our gear.

So, loaded down with tackle and sandwiches, we started our journey which included the double station change and having to stand for half the journey. We finally arrived at Fordingbridge and walked down to the town bridge which spanned the River Avon. We leaned our elbows on the stone wall, looked into the clear water and watched large chub, roach and trout work their way around the bridge supports.

Soon the honk of a horn alerted us to the Brown's van and Ralph's beaming face as he waved to us through the windscreen. The holiday was equally as successful as our previous trip to the Ithon, and the roach and chub were even bigger. The river was running low and clear. Along the stretch were those typical long banks of streamer weed separated by clear gravel runs, and the shoals of fish could be seen, drifting in and out of the protective cover of the weed beds.

After a quick debate, we decided the best method to present our baits would be to float fish and to trot down between the beds of weeds. I had a selection of homemade floats that I had made from swan feathers the previous winter and already tried out on the River Wye. After casting out we would watch the brightly coloured tip of our floats as they trotted down the gravel glides.

They would stop and then shoot under the surface, and with a firm strike, another fat roach or chub would be glided over the landing net. Later in the week we decided to try a different bait, and so early in the morning we collected a quantity of big black slugs. We had a wonderful few hours freelining with these terrific baits. The chub in particular went wild when a slug drifted into their line of vision. On one occasion I had three chub all trying to grab one at the same time. Unfortunately, it was the smallest and fastest that got there first, but it was still a good fish of 3lb 6oz.

This was also the week I caught my first barbel. It was on a day out at Ringwood, Hampshire near the sluice gates. We had been fishing for chub when the barbel grabbed my bait. It weighed 2lb 4oz and took a large piece of bread flake. It was a big surprise for both of us!

We stopped counting the number of chub we caught that week after we reached the half-century. They were all muscular and hard-fighting fish. We also had heavy nets full of prime roach, many over a pound and a quarter. I think it might be worth a sentence or two about the weights of the fish we caught. They may seem relatively small by today's standards as 6lb chub and 2lb roach are regularly reported by fellow anglers. But I believe the sixties were the early years of hunting and targeting particular species of fish. Looking back at the fish we caught, their size and weight were as good as we could have hoped and wished for. We didn't have many sources from which to gather information and learn about up-and-coming techniques.

We relied completely on our logic and abilities.

R eturning to Brum at the end of our week everything seemed to go a bit flat. It was back to one day of fishing a week with our families. Whilst I wouldn't say it was unenjoyable it was just not enough. Mick felt the same. We needed to get more varied adventures out of our weekends. So one of us, I can't remember which, came up with the idea of fishing the local Warwickshire canals. It also made sense because neither of us had yet learnt to drive so we could use the local bus services.

After pouring over Ordinance Survey and BAA club maps we decided to concentrate on the Grand Union Canal at Wootton Wawen not far from Henley-In-Arden. Importantly it was also only a forty-minute bus ride from Mick's house. The plan was for me to go to Mick's after work on Friday, have eggs and chips at his house, and then catch the Midland red bus along Stratford Road to the canal bridge at Wootton Wawen.

There we would camp out on the towpath until mid-day Sunday before making the return bus trips. Our main target would be the bream, plus, if we were lucky, the tench which frequented this stretch of the canal.

We had to walk about 200 metres along the footpath, before arriving with anticipation at our chosen pitch. Arriving early on Friday evening meant there was never another angler in the area we had adopted as 'our pitch'. It was well away from the traffic, close to a small, humped-back bridge, and flanked on either side with high reed beds. Those summer evenings always seemed to be hot and dry and I can't recall ever having to set up our tackle in the rain. We would bait up the pitch with mashed-up bread and maize ground bait and top it off with a few handfuls full of maggots and chopped-up worms. After making up our float rods, we would have a fry-up meal of bacon, eggs, and beans before setting up our bivvy. This consisted of two fishing umbrellas interlocked together and covered with a large sheet of plastic, all pinned down with guide ropes. My old hurricane lamp was then lit and hung onto one of the umbrella's spokes. Our sleeping quarter was another piece of plastic laid out on the towpath's grass verge and held in place with our tackle boxes. We got very proficient at setting up the pitch, and before long our little butane stove would be roaring away, the frying pan sizzling and the smell of browning bacon filling the air. On Fridays we would normally have time for a short evening's session, fishing until we could no longer see our floats. Neither of us worried about what we caught on this first short session because we knew that the Saturday morning would always be rewarding and we were never disappointed.

We'd wake to the sounds of the bird's morning chorus. The mist of dawn would slowly disperse as the rising sun gradually warmed up the day. The canal before us would be bubbling with fish activity. The bream were on the feed, and the light twitching and swaying of the reeds also indicated the presence of our other target fish, tench. Sometimes the resident grass snakes would make an appearance, zigzagging across the canal's surface, and forcing the water voles to scuttle back into their bankside homes.

Making the first cast was thrilling. Float fishing using the lift method and casting into the stream of bubbles, the bites were sometimes instant. They were typical bream bites. The brightly coloured tip of our floats would dip before rising upwards in the water, lay flat, and then after a couple of seconds slide away below the water's surface. We would often cast right against the reeds on the opposite bank. The bites from these areas were far bolder, the float plunging away into the reed stems. These were tench, not big by today's standard, up to about 4lb. Fishing with a 5lb line would normally handle any fish we hooked.

On a couple of occasions Mick got 'broken up' which we thought was due to larger tench, but we found out later there was a small head of carp living in this stretch of canal. We concluded that these were the culprits.

After two to three hours the bites would start to dry up. We would stop fishing, top up the pitch, and let it rest, whilst we had a breakfast fry up. Through the warmer hours of the day, the fishing would be inconsistent and sometimes the pitch would go completely dead. But when the sun descended the pitch came to life again. These Saturday evening sessions could get very hectic. We would fish on well into the dark, then suddenly realise we had not eaten since breakfast. Half asleep with a plate of beef hash and a mug of tea we would sit and relive the day's events. Sunday morning was a repeat performance, except come lunchtime we'd have to pack up to catch the mid-day bus home.

Our final task on a Sunday was to empty the keepnets with care and photograph the weekend's catch, before returning the fish safely, especially the bream. Mick and I have always been keen photographers and between us we have hundreds of slides and photos going back to the early sixties. As we left and walked back along the towpath, we would often wonder whether our pitch would get fished in a Sunday club match, and how it would perform.

Then, one Sunday morning, completely unexpected, an event upset the apple cart and our serene little existence. It's an event that, when we unravel it, still makes us laugh fifty years on.

It was early Sunday morning and we had just finished our usual two hours of frenetic fishing. Mick was still going but I had stopped to cook breakfast. The pan was once again sizzling nicely and the smell of bacon was wafting down the towpath. Whilst buttering bread ready for frying I heard a strange shuffling noise coming from the direction of the small bridge.

Looking up all I could see was a mass of brown and white curved tails coming across the river. Then the yapping and barking started. It was a pack of about twenty hunting hounds. We'd been spotted, and they'd smelt our bacon!

Their reaction was instant and devastating. The hounds charged towards us and straight into our camp. The small stove and frying pan were the first to get smashed. They knocked the stove over whilst snaffling up the bacon, and it rolled down the bank and into the canal. The pan itself was saved from the same fate, but only because two of the hounds had their feet in it, keeping it still whilst they gingerly licked the hot pan clean of melted butter. More hounds were fighting over our bread, ripping the loaves apart. Some were running around with bread stuffed into their mouths. Another group were excitedly nosing through our bait bucket, their feet spilling maggots and worms all across the grass verge. The eggs we were keeping for breakfast got crunched and gobbled down. One individual decided to pee on the umbrella, which triggered a chain reaction with his mates. Now every hound seemed to be cocking a leg. The rods were knocked off their rests, and the lines got tangled around their legs, snapping like cotton. Both rods ended up half submerged in the canal, as well as the landing net. Whilst Mick rescued the ground bait bucket, I shooed the hounds out of our pitch and back down the towpath. The dogs must have been having a great time. First a free breakfast and now a game of chase.

I looked at Michael and he shrugged his shoulders and said something like, "Those frigging dogs, what a frigging mess!". His language was probably stronger. We started cleaning up, making sure nothing of value had been damaged beyond repair. I recovered the stove from the canal but we now had nothing to eat. The dogs had even had our cornflakes!

Then, would you believe it, across the same bridge came what we assumed was the master of the hounds on his horse. He was dressed in a red hunting jacket, white breeches, black hat and black riding boots. Trotting towards us as nice as you like he just said, "Sorry about that chaps," and trotted past, not stopping to show any concern about the mess his pesky dogs had left in their wake. Jasper Carrot would have agreed with the gestures and verbal description we shouted after him.

So did we still enjoy our weekends? Of course we did, it would take a lot more than a pack of hounds and the prospect of meeting them again to stop us from fishing the canal at Wotton Wawen. And luckily, over the next two years, our paths never crossed again. However, it did put a question mark about whether or not we wanted to continue fishing there as regularly as we were. So as the summer started to taper off, we decided it was time to find some 'pastures new'.

As if on cue two key supporting anglers entered our fishing lives. My oldest brother Bob, who sadly died recently long before his time was due, and Bob's university friend Ken Crawford. Both fished together at weekends. But most importantly for Mick and I, both of them had their own transport. This was an absolute blessing for us, and they were very keen to help us get to new locations. And, on occasion, they wanted to join us for a day's fishing.

When Bob and Ken first met they had to use Ken's motor scooter to get places, but carrying fishing tackle on this kind of vehicle was a dicey balancing act. On one occasion, going around a traffic island in Bewdley, Ken took the corner too sharply which resulted in Bob's holdall scraping the road and tipping them both onto the centre reservation. Luckily the grass saved them from any serious injury, but Bob's holdall was ruined.

Whilst Bob's keenness for fishing slowly tailed off, Ken became a firm fishing companion of ours for many seasons. He became a founder member of the South Staffordshire Specimen Group, or SSSG, which Mick and I joined two years later. Bob did fish on and off with us, but I think he mainly did it to be a supportive big brother. Perhaps he could already see that Mick and I had a much greater passion for angling than he did, and he just wanted to help. Thanks, Bob!

Bob's passion was old cars. I can't remember all of them, but my favourites were the Silver Armstrong-Siddeley and the Rover 20, complete with gangster-style running boards. He took us out many times for a day's fishing, normally on the local Midland rivers, including the River Teme, a smaller river that became a firm favourite for some seasons.

On one occasion at Highley on the River Severn, Bob had dropped us off in a bankside field reserved for parking and camping. We were intending to fish for the chub and the new 'in' fish of the mid-seventies, the barbel. Ken had worked with the environmental agency a few years previous, introducing juvenile barbel into the River Severn at Ironbridge.

The weather forecast was not good, sleet and snow, and we were planning to be there for the whole long weekend. But we were still upbeat as I had recently purchased a new green, low-profile two-man ridge tent. This was luxury compared to the now redundant umbrella bivvy. Bob stayed with us until the tent was erected and secure. We checked the stove and stowed away our provisions.

There was a general store on the campsite, so we had only brought the minimum of food as the storage space in the tent was limited. Bob waved his goodbyes, and we were on our own for the next three days. However, over the next few hours, the weather changed and the temperature started to drop dramatically. We fished hard for the chub and barbel, stopping for nourishment when the cold became too severe. The fishing was not a great success, and, due to the deteriorating weather, we were spending more time confined to the tent and consequently getting through our food stock quicker than anticipated. I decided we needed more provisions to get us through the next day and a half. So I walked over the field to the general store. I arrived to find it closed for the weekend!

I trudged back to the tent and informed Mick of the situation, and we did a quick stock check to see what we had left. We had milk and tea, half a packet of digestive biscuits, two slices of bread and two eggs. That was it for the next thirty-six hours. So our evening meal consisted of two eggs and two slices of fried bread, followed thankfully by a cup of steaming tea. (What would we Brits do without a cup of Rosie Lee?) Then, still quite hungry with stomachs half empty, we retired to bed knowing we only had biscuits for breakfast.

To make our situation even more uncomfortable the sleet and snow got heavier. The last sight I saw as I closed the tent flaps was the white flakes getting bigger.

The following morning we looked through the flaps to see a pure blanket of snow across the field. Dragging ourselves out of the tent we had another cup of tea and the biscuits for breakfast, but this just started our juices flowing and we seemed to get hungrier. Bob would not be back until mid-afternoon. We sat in silence, hands tightly curled around our mugs of tea, and stomachs rumbling, discussing whether or not to start fishing.

Then Mick had a flash of genius. The previous day, he had thrown three stale slices of bread out to the birds. We knew the general direction, but skimming bread slices for fun is far more unpredictable than throwing a frisbee. We started crawling around on our hands and knees, scraping away the snow as we went. After a hefty length of time, success! We found two slices of slightly pecked, bent out of shape and rock-hard bread. We started up the stove, melted butter in the pan and gently fried our toast. The wonderful smell made our hunger worse so I quickly covered them with even more butter. Gratefully holding the warm slices of toast we nibbled through our 'gourmet' breakfast.

Bob arrived around three pm, as reliable as ever. Thankfully he had brought snacks for the journey and jokingly lectured us about being better prepared next time. We had scoffed all the snacks by the time we had loaded the car and started home.

Ken was the opposite of Bob about cars. His were always new, big and black. The two I remember were a Ford Zephyr Six and a gigantic Ford Granada Estate big enough to sleep three people, one across the front seats, one across the back seats and the third in the rear behind the back seat. The first time he took us fishing was to Stourport-on-Severn in the autumn of 1965. We spent the day roach fishing the River Severn, near the power station outlets. We caught loads of really good roach, some well over a pound, by float-trotting double maggots. We changed over later to ledgering for the chub. We also started to fish the old yacht basin next to the road bridge in Stourport.

Ken had got into spinning for perch and started to fish around the inlet of the river into the basin, using number three Mepps spinners. Whilst he was spinning Mick and I were either wobbling or float ledgering dead baits up against the sides of the old barges moored in the basin, hoping to catch a pike.

Before long we had caught a couple of small pike. Ken then hooked into a big perch, and, after landing it, we carefully weighed it at 2lb 4oz, by far the biggest perch we had ever seen. After about an hour he caught another perch close to 2lb. Mick and I took it in turns for the next two to three hours trying to emulate Ken's success, but all we caught was a small chub and a perch about half a pound. Over the next two visits to the basin, we caught several good perch plus an occasional small pike, but never anything to match Ken's first fish. Some years later, when Mick was spending a lot of time river fishing for pike, he returned to the basin and caught significantly more pike that were much bigger.

In 1967 we both started to learn to drive. We were determined to pass our driving tests as soon as possible and become unrestricted travellers as we were desperate to find new, unexplored fishing venues. But until that day came Ken continued to ferry us around almost as much as Bob. He introduced us to tench fishing at Walcot Lakes in Shropshire, as well as barbel fishing on the River Avon in and around Christchurch and Sopley. This meant that between Mick's dad and my dad, Ken and Bob, our weekend fishing diaries were always full.

Then an un-missable opportunity arose! My dad was a founder member of a Midlands fishing club called the White Swan Piscatorials or WSP. They had fishing rights on the Rivers Teme, Arrow, Severn, and Lugg, as well as two or three small lakes. Mick and I were invited to apply to the club, and before long we became new members. I am pretty sure my dad's good standing with the committee helped secure our applications. So commenced one of the most enjoyable periods of our early fishing years.

Out again came my two-man tent, re-waterproofed and ready for spring and summer, but now equipped with a new heavy-duty plastic fly sheet. Out also came my trusty butane stove, cooking utensils, kettle and of course the frying pan. With Bob acting as chauffeur for one of the last times, off we went for a week of fishing and camping at Stanford Bridge on the River Teme.

I knew the stretch reasonably well as I had fished it a few times as a junior guest with my dad. In those days there was no barbel in the River Teme, and our stretch was known for its many chub, roach, grayling, trout and very occasional salmon. There was very little angling pressure even at weekends, and the fish lived an undisturbed stress-free existence, and would always feed with confidence.

My favourite pitch at this time was a narrow outcrop of land which extended about a quarter of the way across the river. It formed a natural back swim which was a magnet for big roach, dace and many resident perch. Sadly the pitch no longer exists as one weekend, whilst my mum and I were fishing from it, the end of the outcrop collapsed into the water. It took my mum, who was sitting on her creel at the time, down with it. She fell, bless her, into about six feet of water, but luckily she held onto the creel which kept her afloat as she swam back to the bank. She came ashore right into my pitch, making it easy for me to help her out, but ruining any chances of me catching more roach. A few minutes later she was back on the bank with a couple of towels wrapped around her and her clothes drying in the sun. After a hot cup of tea, and once her clothes were wearable again, she moved to a new spot and carried on fishing.

The recounting of my mum's dipping seems an appropriate time to also mention the unfortunate fishing incidents of my Uncle Harry, whom I referenced at the start of this book. Harry eventually gave up fishing as he kept having accidents. Funny how he always blamed them on George, my dad.

The first incident was when he had gone fishing for bream on the boating lake in Sutton Park, Sutton Coldfield, Birmingham. There you could hire a rowing boat for a small fee. Dad had the boat oars in the rowlocks keeping it steady. Harry had passed all the tackle into the boat and had then gingerly stepped into the unsteady vessel. Dad then realised Harry had left the bait bucket on the wharf, and, huffing and puffing, Harry placed one leg back onto the wharf and reached out to pick up the bucket, but this caused the back end of the boat to move away from the wharf. Being small and round in stature, Harry did the splits and ended up doing the classic boat fall, toppling into the water with his arms flailing. Somehow he managed to cling on to the bait bucket.

On another occasion Dad and Harry were fishing in the late '50s at Ripple on the River Severn from a private landing stage. My Dad had told Harry to leave most of his tackle at the top of the bank because, during these years, large barges navigated up and down producing hefty bough waves. Harry, ignoring Dad as he often did, just carried on fishing. An hour or so later Dad shouted out, "Barge coming," and scrambled up the bank. Harry, due to his aforementioned rotund bulk moved considerably slower. Consequently, he was still sitting on his creel as the wave hit the landing stage. The wave washed across, taking Harry, his creel and all his tackle off into six feet of water. Dad, watching from the safety of the top of the bank, gave him an 'I did warn you' look. Harry managed to grab the end of the landing stage and pull himself to safety, but he lost most of his tackle, rods, creel, landing net, and bait boxes, all of which were now on their way heading downstream towards Tewkesbury.

The third and final time Harry took the plunge was at Bewdley where the banks were steep and often slippery. Dad had cut steps in the bank to get into one of his favourite pitches. For most of the morning, it had rained, and when Dad decided to pack up for lunch he could not get back up the make-shift steps. He called for Harry to pull him up the bank, but as Harry grabbed his hand, Dad slipped back down the steps pulling Harry over his head and somersaulting him into the water. With an almighty cry, Harry disappeared under the surface, only to emerge again, glasses still on his nose and pipe in his mouth.

After that, at Christmas parties and with a few whiskeys in his belly, Dad would re-tell these and other stories. My favourite was the tale of the bull and the stinging nettles. It was a classic Harry tale!

We had just completed the draw for pegs at a club match on the River Severn. Getting to the pegs involved walking past a field, then over a stile and then across a narrow plank spanning a ditch. The weather was changeable and a shower had just ceased. Harry did not fancy crossing the stile or the plank and he dallied at the back of the queue. Everyone had crossed safely when suddenly someone noticed Harry was motoring as fast as his little legs would carry him across the field. Also motoring, chasing and easily gaining on Harry was a very large black bull.

Harry had ditched his creel and fishing rods by the time he reached a gate in the corner of the field. Not waiting to unbolt it, and with the bull's snorts bearing down on him, he hurtled the gate, clearing it in fine style. But unknown to Harry as he leapt into the air, directly below him was the ditch and a bed of stinging nettles. With a curse and a shout of alarm, he fell full stretch into it. Ouch! Getting him out was difficult and time-consuming. It resulted in a late start to the match and many grumbles from the other anglers.

Consequently, and not surprisingly, Harry stopped going fishing.

Anyway, back to mine and Mick's week of fishing on the River Teme. The first upstream bend above Stanford Bridge included an extensive set of rapids. We called this the lower meadow. The middle stretch leading eventually to the hop fields was the middle meadow and consisted of a mixture of shallow runs and deeper pools and glides. The spinney or top stretch consisted largely of long shallow bends with steep overhanging banks and large dangling willows.

I expect this whole stretch of river has changed dramatically over the last forty years and I wonder how the contours of the bottom have altered. At the time our bank of the river was four to six feet deep, but halfway across there was a shelf where it deepened by another one to two feet. I decided, early the next morning, to wade over to the drop-off and, with the aid of my landing net handle, I worked my way down the stretch. As I went I discovered many hiding places where the shelf's undercut provided hidden protection for the shoals of roach and chub.

This time spent mentally mapping the river's contours helped us during our many visits to identify where to find the better shoals and in particular the larger chub. It was especially useful for Mick, who out-fished me big time, catching both a 4lb 2oz and a 4lb 4oz chub. Regularly baiting up a couple of pitches with mashed-up bread, he had some terrific catches by alternating from one to the other. I, on the other hand, preferred to sight fish and stalk the chub I wanted to catch. I spent most of my time wandering along our stretch of the Teme, freelining bread flake. Armed with my polaroids, rod, landing net and a thick-sliced white loaf, I would find a likely-looking swim and cast across the flow watching the line as it entered the water, waiting for a sharp tap or a slack line bite. Sometimes I would select one particular chub and wait as it engulfed the slowly sinking bread flake drifting past its nose.

On occasions, when it was a hot cloudless day, we would change over to dry fly fishing. Our favourite flies for the chub consisted of imitation horseflies, blue bottles, moths and the irresistible mayfly. We even tried with some success imitation caterpillars and various grubs. Most of these patterns Mick and I tied during the close season. If you get the opportunity to dry fly fish for chub, believe me, it is a very exciting and rewarding experience.

We would present the fly so that it drifted with the current, under the overhanging bushes or trees. Out of the shadows would appear a big fat chub, sometimes two or three, and normally there was no messing about. The first chub to reach the fly would greedily suck it down between those thick white lips, then turn around and head for its lair. Strike too quickly and there was a good chance the hook would not get a stronghold, causing the chub to spook and scatter any others in the vicinity far and wide. If everything went to plan, and the first fish was quietly landed, there was a very good chance of catching a second and sometimes a third before they wised up.

It was not only chub we caught on the fly rods, we also had some good-sized brown trout and beautiful grayling. The occasional trout supplemented our evening meals, but never the 'lady of the stream' as my Dad used to call the grayling.

We don't know exactly how many chub we caught from the Teme at Stanford Bridge, but it would not be unusual to catch forty to fifty over a long weekend.

We were comparing notes not so long ago during one of our regular weekend telephone calls, and we concluded that our success was not due to extraordinary skill but due to us fishing differently than most of the other anglers we knew. Whenever we could we'd put aside the traditional tactic of sitting in one pitch for long hours. It was about travelling light and being mobile, keeping on the move until we found the fish. It's a tactic Mick and I still use some fifty years later, irrespective of the species of fish we're endeavouring to catch.

The land we camped on at Stanford Bridge belonged to a nearby farm owned by the Spareys. We got to know farmer Pete Sparey and his family well over the next couple of seasons. More than once we had Sunday dinner with them in exchange for doing jobs around the farm. Their oldest son, Anton, would wander down to the river, and he would sit and talk with us as we fished. Sometimes he would bring down his canoe and we would spend time gliding down the Teme inspecting the river's contours. We would always let him have a go with one of our rods, but before long he would have to drag himself away to complete his list of farm chores.

We fished and camped at Stanford Bridge whenever we could find a free weekend and a driver. It became our favourite 'go-to' place for two to three years. Occasionally, on an extended stay, we would hang up our rods and help Anton guide the cow herd down to the milking sheds. Lots of us anglers have, at one time or another, encountered inquisitive cows. Now seems like the right time to relay our unfortunate incident with Pete's prime herd of milkers.

The weekend of the incident started quietly enough. Bob had once again been our driver. He pulled his Rover 20 onto the grass verge next to the metal gate leading down into the middle field. I walked the short distance back to the farm and checked with Pete where the cows were grazing as we wanted to camp in the middle field close to the river. He confirmed that the cows would be grazing in the top spinney for the next few days out of our way, and permitted us to camp close to the hedgerow in the middle field. After driving over the field, unloading our gear, waving Bob off and securing the gate, we set up camp under a large overhanging tree next to the hedgerow. The two-man ridge tent with its super new waterproof flysheet, and the protection provided by the hedge and tree, meant we would stay warm and dry. Irrespective of a change in the weather we were confident that we would be snug and warm.

The following morning, after an early breakfast, we started fishing at the top end of the club's stretch of the river. We intended to work our way down through the spinney and finish at our camp in the middle field around lunchtime. We spotted the cows as soon as we started fishing, they were all crowded around the five-bar metal gate leading to the middle field. Not paying too much attention to them, we carried on working downstream stalking and catching the chub as we came across their hiding places.

After about four hours we had worked our way back to the bankside stile leading to the middle field, congratulating ourselves on another successful, fun-filled chubbing session. Climbing the stile we both froze. There, surrounding our campsite, was Pete's herd of cows. We charged across the grass shouting and waving our arms and our fishing rods in their general direction.

At first the otherwise occupied cows took no notice, but as we got closer one or two started to reluctantly trot off. The remainder of the herd just turned their heads, stared at us and then carried on munching away at whatever they had managed to grab. We were now very close, and as I got to the first cow, in desperation, I whacked it across the backside with my rod. It was like hitting a rock with a feather. With lots more arm waving, shouting and swearing we eventually pushed and forced them out of our campsite. Like a bunch of naughty children they trotted off across the field, snorting and mooing their displeasure.

Our campsite looked more like a bomb site. It was much worse than the hound incident at Wotton Wawen.

My tent's new flysheet had been chewed to pieces, and it was covered in slobber from their inquisitive elongated tongues. Later Pete told us, "Cows go ballistic for the taste of plastic." They had trampled the tent flat and broken one of the tent poles. They'd snapped and dislodged the pegs and guide ropes. Once again our box of food supplies had been completely demolished, the milk cartons bitten, sucked dry then discarded all over the field. My beloved butane gas stove was ruined by a cow's hoof. The long-suffering frying pan had been kicked and dented and was left sticking out of the hedge. One of my Wellington boots was missing and I never saw it again. And everywhere, and I do mean everywhere, there were piles of smelly, steaming cow dung. The rucksacks and spare tackle bags were covered in it and cow saliva, as was the flattened tent.

We had nothing to eat or drink and no tent. Our sleeping bags were useable but ripped. But with luck, most of the spare fishing tackle was fine because we had tucked it under the hedgerow for security.

Caps in hand we went to the Sparey's farmhouse for help. When Pete heard of our predicament he realised he was to blame. Unfortunately, he had forgotten to mention to Anton that we were camping in the middle field. Unaware, Anton had moved the herd from the spinney to give them better grazing in the middle field. This was why the cows had been crowded around the gate earlier in the day, they had already eyeballed our tent!

So the herd had certainly got their 'better grazing'. Their change of diet consisted of our tent, our food and lots of plastic! Pete and his wife Margaret felt very responsible, and as a gesture of goodwill not only put us up for the remainder of the holiday but also fed us at mealtimes. We were able to do some temporary repairs to the tent but happily accepted their invitation as the sky was threatening rain.

Bob, as usual, arrived on time unaware of our problems. He was surprised to see us sitting on the farmyard wall as he drove over the bridge. Mick and I decided there and then we would pay the Spareys back for their kindness. We decided to help whenever we could around the farm. Mostly we collected eggs from the two thousand chickens and loaded hay bales onto the low loaders when necessary. So started a strong friendship with the Sparey family, which lasted up to the autumn of 1973 when my wife Carol and I moved to New Zealand. Peter Sparey passed away in 2016 at the age of 89. I still often think of him and his wonderful family.

Being novice farm hands it was easy for the Spareys to pull our legs when we helped out. One glorious summer day we were asked to move some bales of hay. Pete directed us to a large stack of bales at the bottom of the field where an empty trailer was waiting to be filled. Pitch forks in hand we energetically started loading them onto the flatbed.

The mid-day sun got hotter and we got slower and sweatier. Mick said, pointing to the Sparey family working at the top of the field, " I thought we were fit John, but look at their trailer, it's almost full. We will be another couple of hours yet." With a grunt, heads down, we carried on. Eventually we finished and dragged our bodies back to the farmhouse.

The following morning, over breakfast, Pete with a big grin came clean and informed us that the bails we had loaded were heavier than theirs. The moisture in the grass was to blame, as it had worked its way downhill and seeped into the hay bales. They'd had a bet that we would not finish our task, so I suppose no one won.

The summer evenings always seemed sunny and long, which meant we often fished on well into the dark.

I had a couple of amusing wildlife encounters after dusk fell. I was once sitting quietly next to my plastic ground bait bucket when it started to tip up and move slightly to one side. Picking up my torch I gently lifted the side of the bucket and shone the beam underneath. I could just make out a small mound of earth and in the middle a little black snot followed by two tiny, clawed hands. It was a mole. I expect it was wondering why breaking through the earth was so difficult.

The second encounter was when I was walking along a high section of the bank. I heard snuffles and odd noises coming from the river to my right and looking over the edge of the bank I saw a family of badgers playing close to the water's edge. They were sliding down the bank, sometimes on their bellies, sometimes on their backs, like they were playing on a muddy playground slide. Each time they'd stop just short of the water, gamboling and sprinting back up the bank for another go. They were so engrossed in their game that they took no notice of me.

Mick and I didn't fish together every weekend. Now and then we would have a break from each other and spend a day fishing with other friends, family or even on our own. However, it was always good to meet up again and with gleeful anticipation plan our next outing. I can honestly say we have never had a serious argument or falling out, and now, after knowing each other for so long, I can't see why that would ever change. It was during the coarse fishing close season that Mick and I intended to fish separately. Mick would have the opportunity to salmon fish with his Dad and Uncle Arthur on the Wye, and I purchased a salmon licence so I could fish the WSP stretch at Holt Fleet on the River Severn. The stretch extended from below the weir down to the road bridge. The salmon were few and far between.

The first year I only saw one on the bank caught by an elderly gentleman. It weighed 10lb, and I still have the photograph I took of him holding his prize catch.

For my efforts, I only had a good-sized brown trout at the end of the first year and a couple of 3lb chub. Then, during a dull day at the start of my second salmon season, I had a very hard pull while fishing just under the weir. My Mepps spinner had been seized by something that felt substantial. Suddenly this solid object took off downstream leaping clear of the water. I could see it was a large silver sided salmon.

My old Mitchell reel screamed in protest as it continued towards the bridge passing two other anglers on the way. There was a sloped shingle bank downstream from me which I scrambled along, trying to keep in touch with my potential prize catch. With my Mark 4 Stepped Up carp rod bent double I started to gain line and was soon parallel with the salmon. Then, suddenly, it changed direction and dived straight under my bank and into a tangle of tree roots! Another arm-wrenching tug and it was gone, leaving my spinner snagged in the roots, but not before I saw a flash of silver as it shot off again towards the road bridge.

Now I knew there was a deep holding pool under the bridge which was not fished very often as it was full of snags and lost lures. My thinking was that the salmon would be looking for a quiet location where it could recover, so taking a chance I decided to give it a go. Cautiously I cast my Mepps spinner across the flow under the bridge arch, allowing it to swing in towards my bank. As I gently started to retrieve it, it was immediately grabbed by a very angry fish twisting and turning. Line grating against unseen snags I bullied the fish into the landing net. At the time I had my doubts about it being a salmon, the fight was different with more head shaking and short runs, and it didn't feel so powerful. Looking into the net my thoughts became reality.

It was a decent pike of exactly 11lb, but not the salmon as I hoped. Any other time I would have been very pleased but not this time. I was so close but not close enough. Oh well, such is life.

Before the start of the salmon season at Holt Fleet, the WSP would organise a 'bank clearing party'. Mick and I decided to attend with our driver for the day, our friend Ken Crawford. It was a wet day, the banks were slippery, and as we arrived work had already commenced. Several wood-burning fires were smoking and spitting defiantly at the drizzling rain.

Some members of the working party were drinking tea and keeping warm while awaiting instructions. Being the youngest adults and eager to please whilst the more mature helpers lingered, we quickly joined the nearest group and were soon split into two working parties. Ken went off with the tree-cutting party as he had a brand new bow saw to try out. Both Mick and I went with the chopping and collection group, gathering dead wood and branches, and clearing up the bank side. This also meant we had the opportunity to stop and warm our hands by the bonfire. The river was running high and coloured, and we were being as careful and safe as we could, working steadily along the steep bank. Suddenly we were interrupted by an alarm call, one of the tree-cutting team had fallen into the river. Everyone rushed over, slipping and sliding into the gathering crowd. And in the middle of the crowd was a very wet and somewhat shocked-looking Ken.

He had been helping to remove an old, unsafe tree which was hanging over the raging water. One long branch in particular needed cutting off so Ken, with safety rope firmly secured around his waist and his new bow saw at the ready, started to inch his way along the offending branch. Of course it suddenly snapped in two, plunging Ken six feet vertically downwards. Fortunately, he had only been submerged up to his waist as his fall had been stopped by a second branch which was level with the surface of the water. It saved him from a complete soaking and a fall that could easily have ended up with a more tragic result. But he had landed astride the second branch, so not only with his pride dented but also his unmentionables. It was hot tea and a warm blanket by the fire for Ken, plus the knowledge that we would be ribbing him whenever possible about his bank-clearing expertise. The good news was that his new bow saw caught on a smaller branch and had been retrieved.

Back to December 1967, and the early days of my driving lessons. Mick too had started. My Dad took me out for my first lesson in his green column change Ford Consul. It was all going well until we got to a steep hill and I forgot what gear I was in. Panicking, and not able to find any gear, I coasted down the hill and around a sharp right-hand bend straight into a line of metal dustbins. Dad was not amused, and after hauling on the handbrake he made me pick up the spilt rubbish. I also got a tongue-lashing for denting the Consul's front bumper. The damage was a constant reminder every time I got in the car until the day he finally swapped it for a new Ford Cortina.

Now starting to earn a decent weekly wage and eager to get my own car I signed up for proper driving lessons. Dad's assistance ended and I started lessons with the BSM school of motoring. After twenty sweaty one-hour lessons I nervously took my driving test and failed. But with further encouragement and five more lessons I passed in April 1968. I celebrated by throwing my L plates into the nearest rubbish bin.

Before long, with help from Dad's contacts, I purchased a grey Ford Thames 7cwt van from a workmate. What a great vehicle it turned out to be, very reliable, economical, and robust. It was ideal for all our fishing tackle and camping gear, big enough to sleep in if required, very secure and easy to drive.

I rang Mick and told him the good news. No more would I be relying on others for lifts, and before long we were discussing how and where we could test out my new vehicle, reg 864 PEA. We had a four-day holiday coming up, and little did we realise that this trip was going to set the mould for the rest of our fishing years.

We decided, instead of spending the time pleasure fishing on the Teme, that we needed to push ourselves forward. We needed to set and achieve new fishing goals. We chose to head out of the Midlands and find a day ticket venue in the South West. At some point we had heard about an unspoilt water in Devon which was reported to have excellent pike fishing opportunities. Mick was as eager as anything as this was the dream holiday for him, and with gentle pressure I agreed that this would also be the ideal test for the van.

Maybe this trip was the true start of Mick's passion for pike. It was a truly memorable adventure and the location was Slapton Ley in South Devon. The lake is a bird sanctuary so bank fishing was not allowed, but it was possible to hire one of the available rowing boats. Sadly the Ley's fishing has dramatically declined over the years due to water pollution. Mick refers to this in his book *Fishing for Pike and Predators*. Late on the Friday evening of our holiday I picked Mick up from his house and we set off down the new M5 heading south. Travelling through the night we arrived at Slapton Sands and parked up in a layby next to the Ley.

As the dawn broke the light from the slowly rising sun not only spread its red glow across the sea but also across the still waters of the Ley. I drove the van around to the boat house, parked up and walked down the path to pay for our day tickets. We received advice about the hot spots on the Ley from the bailiff, and before long we had loaded the small rowing boats with our tackle and pushed off onto the calm clear water. Gently we rowed and glided the small boat out of the channel and past the reed beds into more open water. We drifted with the breeze over shoal after shoal of rudd and perch.

Some of the shoals were huge, and on the fringes of the constantly moving masses, we could see familiar long dark shapes in the deeper water. Pike! We spent a couple of hours exploring the edges and would occasionally see the snout of other pike sticking through the reeds. Eventually, we came across a large bay surrounded on three sides by the reeds but with many small islands dotted in its perimeters. We immediately named this the Bay of Islands and it quickly became clear to us that this seemed to be a magnet area for the shoals of rudd and perch. At this point though we did not know why.

Concentrating on this bay for the first two days fishing we would float fish for a good hour, catching mainly rudd and making them splash as much as possible to stir up the pike. Once we spotted a pike moving into the area we'd put out the float-fished dead baits. We would normally end up with a few pike before they moved off. Then we would work the rowboat around the small islands using spinners and lures as well as having a dead bait drifting behind the boat. We caught dozens of perch on the spinners and lures, and now and then, as our dead baits drifted close to the reeds, a pike would shoot out and snatch one.

There were times when we just had to stop fishing and rest up, eating our sandwiches and washing them down with hot coffee from our flasks with our feet up. Sharing jokes with a best friend takes some bettering.

One lunchtime I was in the process of munching on a cheese and pickle roll when Mick whispered to me to stay still and not to turn around. I could see a ripple running across the water surface, and then I felt a sharp tap in the middle of my back. I automatically jumped and spun and there, leaning over the stern of the boat, was a rather large swan. In fright, it hissed at me. Mick suggested I give it a piece of my roll which I promptly did. The swan crunched it up and with the help of a little water gulped it down, then it came back for more. "I'll never get rid of it now," I growled at Mick.

"Try him on a bit of pickle," Mick laughingly replied. I did, and to my pleasant surprise, the swan shook its head, flapped its wings, and swiftly glided away.

Towards the evening Mick and I would reposition the rowboat into the channel by the boat house. The channel of water separated our lake from a smaller private lake. We had discovered that the massive shoals of rudd and perch frequently travelled from one lake to the other, but as evening shadows lengthened the majority of the shoals left the smaller lake moving through the channel into the Ley. The pike knew of this migration and would always be waiting in a semi-circle ready to pounce on the approaching shoals of fish. They would hammer into the passing packs, scattering them high and wide, silver sides flashing until the last rays of the sun dipped behind the surrounding hills.

But it was also our turn to ambush the pike. It didn't matter if we used spinners, lures or dead baits we had constant sport until night fell. Finally, with aching arms, it was time to vacate. None of the pike were big. I had one which made 10lb 4oz, but for us novices it was a wonderful experience repeated every evening we fished the Ley.

If I remember correctly we landed fifteen pike between us on that first visit and lost about the same amount through striking too quickly. We lost count of the number of spinner caught perch. Over the next three years we fished the Ley five times, on every occasion using the same tactics, and we were always rewarded with very satisfying results.

However, as Mick quoted in one of his books, "When I think back on it, how naïve we were and how much better we could have fished, I could almost despair." But we all have a starting point. We were learning something new every time we went to a venue or fished for a new species. There were very few anglers available or prepared to assist our early efforts so we had to forge ahead on our own. In today's angling world there is an endless amount of reading materials and videos to entertain and learn from. It can be relatively easy for a newcomer to catch a very big fish in a short space of time. I have no problem with this, you can call it progress, but I believe our early adventures held more mystique.

May 1968 was passing quickly and it wouldn't be long before the new coarse fishing season would officially be on us. With this in mind a new challenge formulated in our minds. The 15th of June saw us travelling in the van due west into Shropshire, to fish for Tench at Wolcot Lakes. We would be there for two days and hoped that only a few other anglers would have the same idea.

The lakes were situated on the grounds of a country estate and separated by a private road leading to a stately home. The BAA had the fishing rights on one side of the lakes. We entered the estate through the imposing gates, drove down the driveway and pulled up in the allocated parking area. We unloaded and proceeded to walk down the well-worn path which led to the water's edge. We passed a number of likely-looking pitches, before finding two situated next to each other, both fringed with bank-side reeds.

We were in luck as there were only a couple of other anglers looking for pitches, and we were comfortable with our choices. After sorting tackle and settling in there was nothing left to do but wait until midnight and the first cast of the new season. We settled back on our bed chairs, drinking tea and eating bacon sandwiches, watching the sun go down.

As dusk arrived the water voles appeared. These busy, inquisitive little fellows would peep out of the reeds and watch us eat. We used to take it in turns to balance a piece of bread on the top of our wellies and tempt a vole to snatch it. If we moved our feet just a little bit the cute rodents would leap back into the water, sometimes doing an impressive backflip. Ten out of ten for form.

It wasn't long after the voles went home that the resident bats arrived. The air became thick with them, swooping and diving across the surface of the lake, feeding on any insect that took their fancy. One evening I accidentally hit one as I was casting out. I felt the thud and then Mick found the poor little fellow stunned but alive in the grass. It spent the night gently wrapped up in my hat, and by dawn, it had vanished. I hope it found its way back to its mates.

Although fishing with maggots and bread flake for the tench worked, we were being constantly pestered by roach and perch. We decided a change of bait was necessary so the next time we fished Wolcot we used worms exclusively, either chopped or whole, and mixed them into a groundbait of tuna and mashed bread. It worked well for the tench and we started catching bigger and more plentiful fish. It almost eliminated the rudd but unfortunately not the perch, and now we had further issues with eels and pike. The pike in particular surprised us, and over the next three sessions we caught dozens of them using bundles of garden worms.

Eel populations were in abundance during the 1960s and, on various occasions early in the season, we fished Wolcot exclusively for them. Using a wire trace helped eliminate the smaller perch and made landing the pike far safer as it ensured no

bite-offs. We enjoyed some exceptional eel fishing sessions and it would not be unusual to catch more than a dozen over a weekend. The best was over 3lb. Mick was in his element, fishing for what soon became another of his favourite predators.

One of the biggest problems we encountered in our early eel fishing days was how to keep them all together overnight, ready for a photo shoot the following morning. These slippery critters were a real handful! They'd hide in the long grass or try to search out the nearest route back to the water. Can you imagine a dozen eels all on the bank at the same time, slithering and wriggling through clenched hands?

We came up with various solutions to keep them safe and secure. Our first method was to use a conventional keep net but unfortunately, when we lifted the net, all of the eels had escaped through a hole in the mesh. The keep nets in the 70s were nowhere near as strong as today, so we guessed the eels had found a weak spot and burrowed through. Our second attempt was to use a plastic dustbin and half sink it into the water, but the eels always managed to slither up the sides. We'd hear them plopping back into the watery depths, occasionally tipping the bin over as they took flight.

Our final and best solution was to use the wire mesh wastepaper bins that we found on the path leading down to the lake. They were strong enough to prevent the eels from burrowing out, heavy

enough to sink and stay upright in the water easily, and they had a lip along the top which deterred any escapee. However, we still lost a few and eventually, we concluded that eels were just very slippery customers. We would always wash out the mesh waste bins before and after use and carefully return them to their original location on our way back to the van.

Years later in 2021, Carol and I visited Mick and Jan on their boat on the River Nene. The first thing Mick greeted me with were two eels, with one around about 2lb. He just happened to have caught them whilst waiting for us to arrive. Not bad for a couple of hours fishing on a bright summer day.

As summer pushed into Autumn we returned to Wolcot Lakes. Equipped with our spinning gear we caught even more pike and many good-sized perch. It became clear to me that I would always be an angler, happy to catch any variety of fish, but Mick was becoming more and more fascinated by the predator species, and in particular pike.

I feel that the 1960s was an important period for angling. Whilst Mick and I bumbled along, maybe sometimes thinking we were better than we were, there were other more experienced anglers going about their fishing business that were learning lots and catching more.

We needed to smarten up our game, especially for catching pike.

Through the winter we extensively experimented with various pike fishing techniques by refining our baits and rigs. Then in January 1969 Mick and I were invited to join the South Staffordshire Specimen Group, or the SSSG as it became known. Consequently, we began getting recognition for our dedication to the pursuit of specific fish species, and we now had the chance to exchange and discuss ideas with other like-minded anglers. It encouraged us to re-focus on what we want to achieve from fishing.

So from that point on we adopted a flexible yearly calendar.
- Autumn and winter – pike, perch, and chub
- Spring – eels
- Late spring and summer - barbel, chub, and the now in-vogue fish, carp!

Well into winter, with many rivers in flood and bursting their banks, we found ourselves searching for a suitable river to pike fish. We eventually settled on a two-hour drive due west to the River Arrow. The WSP club had a couple of stretches on this river. Its fast-running, clear waters and gravel bottom meant the excess water ran off quickly. The Arrow is known for its grayling and I had previously fished it several times with my dad.

Along one stretch is a small tributary called the Little Arrow. It's not much deeper than four feet and in places almost narrow enough to jump over. When the river was high, and running at full pelt, lots of fish took to holding up in this tributary, including pike. Quietly creeping to the water's edge, where the entrance joined the main river, we would excitedly toss a coin for the first cast.

Whoever won had the opportunity to gently swing out a fresh dead bait, normally a spratt, suspended under a pike bung. The first take was almost always instant, and once hooked the pike would take off into the main river, hug the bank and head downstream. They would twist and turn using the current to their advantage and test our cane and fibreglass rods to the limit. Fighting long and hard eventually they were netted and, after being unhooked, left in a landing net to recover.

Then it would be the turn of the loser of the coin toss to have the next cast, and the process would be repeated. Sometimes we would take three or four pike from the entrance pitch, and then move onto the next pool a little higher up the tributary. We caught nothing in double figures, but it did help instil in both of us the importance of location and opportunity. Bigger and better pike would soon start coming to our rods, but for now, the enjoyment and excitement of another new challenge was the important thing. We felt we were fishing as well as we could with the resources and tackle we had available. In the late '60s we were still using pike bungs which were split down the side and needed a peg to wedge the line to the required depth. These bungs had their uses as it was a simple matter of removing the peg and pulling the line out of the slot to change from float fishing to fishing sink and draw, or free line a dead bait. However, if the water was over seven feet deep, casting out a fixed pike bung became difficult and often ended in tangles or bad presentation.

One weekend we were fishing a deep lake at Bretby Pools near Buton-on-Trent and found it too deep to use a fixed bung. The weather was cold and with a steady breeze blowing we were struggling to get our baits down to where we thought the pike would be lining up. Towards the late afternoon, another angler caught a 9lb pike. We wandered over to see his catch, and he explained that due to the very deep water, it was necessary to get the baits close to the bottom. He was kind enough to show us his pike rigs and explained how he always used a fixed paternoster, which presented his live roach close to the bottom. After thanking him, and hectically sorting through my tackle box for something to make a makeshift rig, I changed over to a primitive paternoster rig. It was a method new to me, by no means perfect but good enough. As darkness fell and we were getting ready to pack up my pike float disappeared and I ended the day netting a nice pike of 11lb 2oz, my biggest pike for that winter.

I continue to use paternosters occasionally, but most of my pike fishing has been done on rivers so a more conventional sliding float satisfies my needs. However, if you get a chance to read Mick's latest book *Great Pike Fishing Days* published in 2021, he has a whole chapter explaining the merits of the paternoster rigs and variations. As you would expect he backs up his explanations with some extraordinary big pike catches.

Springtime 1968 arrived, and with Mick now having his own Ford Cortina, we could come and go as we wished, meeting at a chosen location and only picking each other up as and when we wanted.

Our eel fishing had become more productive because as well as Wolcot we'd found a better lake not far from Earlswood Lakes. It produced bigger eels. Mick landed the pick of the bunch with a 5lb 8oz brute. My personal best was just over 4lb.

Constantly fishing for eels and using mainly worms, requires a lot of bait. So where did we get a constant source of fresh earthworms? The answer was from the local parks. It was not outlawed then, so a day or two before we went eeling I would pick Mick up in the van and we would drive to a park. Armed with buckets and torches we would start hunting through the park's grassed areas. On a good night, the worms would be lying out on the damp grass, half in and half out of their holes. With a gentle tug, they could be captured, and they'd be in the bucket before they knew what happened. But occasionally, especially with a big fat worm, they would sense a movement and instantly retreat down their hole. Grab them too tight and the result was always half a worm, which never lasted long when left in the bucket. Pulling them nice and easy proved to be the winning method. A successful night would see us get a third of a bucket of fresh wriggling worms in a couple of hours.

One evening, whilst deeply involved in worming, we were disturbed by two police officers. They must have seen the beams from our torches and thought we were up to no good. They came over to investigate, asking what we had in the bucket. They shone their torches onto the mass of slimy worms.

The officers were not convinced that worming was all we were up to. One officer asked where we lived. Mick, being a local, was fine, but maybe I should have lied instead of telling him truthfully that I came from Winston Green. He gave me a look which said he knew there was a maximum-security prison at Winston Green. His next question was, "Is that your grey van by the park gate? What's the make and registration number?" Well, do you think I could remember the registration? "It's a Ford" I stuttered, "864…". For the life of me, I could not remember the rest. Luckily, my mate Mick came to the rescue. "864 PEA," he quickly replied. This took the heat out of the situation.

While one officer went to check the van the second officer continued to peer into the bucket. "What have you got these for anyway?" he asked turning his nose up at the slivering mass. "Fishing." replied Mick, "Eel fishing." The officer now looked convinced, and said his goodbyes, but not before telling us to hurry along in case they got complaints. Mick pulled my leg repeatedly after that about not remembering my van's number.

Both Mick and I had car accidents in '68. Mick rolled his car, not long after he purchased it, on a fishing trip. He did extensive damage and needed four new wings and two new suspension units for his much-loved Ford Cortina. He was also carrying half a bucket of worms which managed to deposit themselves all over the road. Dazed from the crash Mick spent some time picking them up and returning them to the bucket. Big fat worms were a valued commodity and not to be forsaken easily.

My accident was a bit more bazaar. The story starts about three weeks before the actual day of the crash. We had been fishing in particularly wet and windy conditions and had stowed two pints of maggots in the back of my van. Unfortunately, a leaking roof vent allowed the driving rain to breach my vehicle and run into our bait boxes. So on returning, after a fairly unproductive day's fish, we of course opened the van's back door and were greeted by a wavy line of crawling larvae. They were all over the van floor and up the sides. Right over the front seats they stretched, head to toe, as if off to some secret location. For the next week, I kept finding little groups of the blighters, especially under the carpets. You can imagine my delight when finally I thought I had captured the last escapees.

Roll on to two weeks later. I had been worming and had collected almost one hundred of them. Early the following morning I loaded them into the van with my tackle. I was setting off to meet Mick once again. It was a cold day, much colder than the last few, and whilst waiting in a queue at road works I switched on the heater and blower. Suddenly the windscreen and dashboard were covered in big black flies. They were sluggish, I imagine partly due to the fact they'd just been unexpectedly launched through the air vents. They didn't fly around at all, they just meandered and buzzed and wandered across the dashboard. They were, of course, the remainder of the maggots, now hatched and maturing. Brushing the windscreen while winding down the window, I started hand-shovelling the critters along the dashboard and out the driver's window.

Glancing up I could see the traffic was now moving so I changed into second gear and started steadily forward. But I was still distracted by the flies and suddenly there was a dull thump and the van ground to a halt. I had hit the Vauxhall Estate in front of me. I'd failed to notice him stop again for the road works.

Opening the door to say it was my fault, I was joined by a steady trickle of escaping flies taking off into the sky and it must have looked quite horrid.

The estate's back bumper was a right off and so was its boot lid. We exchanged details and with his boot tied down with an old piece of string, the driver trundled up the road, his bumper occasionally scrapping along the tarmac.

With my dad's help, a heavy lump hammer and a pair of long blacksmith forge tongues, we were able to straighten my front bumper, and I was still able to go fishing with Mick for the day. And you know, the driver of the estate never did make an insurance claim. On second thoughts the driver had seemed very reluctant to let me look inside his boot. It had been crammed full of square cardboard boxes. Mick's imagination, or maybe logic, suggested that the estate owner may have been transporting illegally obtained black-market items or dodgy 'ripped-off' men's shoes. I just thought he was just a salesperson having a bad day. We never did get to know, as for me my van repairs came to less than a fiver.

E el fishing once more took up the majority of our time leading to the start of the 1968 coarse fishing season, but we yet again wanted some sort of new challenge. Good fortune came to our rescue. The WSP club had obtained the fishing rights to Shobden Lakes near Leominster in Shropshire. It was a small complex set on a pig farm, and it consisted of two lakes and a third which was locally called the Duck Pond. Newly dug it had been stocked with mirror and common carp to about 8lb. The first weekend we fished it I caught twenty-two carp, and I guess Mick caught a similar amount. Once again it became too easy to catch the naive fish. On the second visit, we did equally as well on the two stock pools. However, Ken Crawford fished the Duck Pond instead and caught a genuine wild carp of 3lb plus. Neither Mick nor I knew what 'wildies' were then. It was a new species.

So the following weekend we all met late Friday evening at Shobden Lakes and after a good night's sleep were up bright and early Saturday morning, excited to look at the duck pond. It was shaped like a banana and very shallow, but we did see a good head of wild carp basking in the morning sun underneath the floating weed.

We fished through the day catching the odd fish up to 4lb on bread flake and worms. Mick did hook something different on a bunch of worms which zigzagged its way through the reed bed and finally broke him. We suspect it was a big eel. Things were getting interesting. Then Ken lost a bigger carp, again in the reeds, and we realised we were fishing with too light a line. So for the remainder of the weekend, we moved back to the easier lake and finished the weekend catching a load more carp, up to 6lb, and got sunburnt in the process.

That week we re-spooled our reels and before long were ready to fish the Duck Pond for a third time. It is true to say that these carp went wild when hooked, shooting off like rockets, stirring up the silt bottom of the pond with their tails, and forever embedding themselves in the reed beds. On a further visit to Shobden, Mick and I were joined by another new member of the SSSG, Roger Pitt. For three years we regularly fished Shobden hoping to catch a specimen wildie of 5lb. I was very close in 1970 with a fish that weighed 4lb 14oz, but it was Roger who finally did the deed in 1971 with a smashing wildie of 5lb 6oz! Mick, well, although he enjoyed catching the wildies, I think that he was hoping a big eel would make an appearance and grab his cocktail of worms.

On one of our visits to Shobden, I decided to fish the very last pitch at the far end of the Duck Pond. It was the deepest and darkest part of the pond, always in the shade and overhung with willows. The water looked eerie as I baited up with bread mash, and a thick mist had started to descend from the surrounding hills.

It was only Mick and I fishing on this occasion, and I had rejoined him for our late supper before the night session. We got talking about ghosts and things that go bump in the night. Mick told me there was supposed to be an unearthly monk who haunted a nearby derelict church. With these thoughts in the back of my mind, I picked up my gear, wished Mick tight lines, and walked in the semi-darkness to my pitch at the end of the pond. Casting out to the baited area by the reeds on the opposite bank, my free-lined bread flake slowly sank out of view and rested on top of the silt bottom. Gently tightening up to the rod tip, I opened the bail arm and slipped my silver paper indicator over my line. The evening's air was so still it hung stationary. Up went the umbrella and I lay down, full length, under its limited protection, my head slightly raised on my waterproofs.

The darkness had now fully arrived, but I was determined not to put on my torch, and my eyes had started to adjust to the night. The atmosphere became thick and still, the mist rolling around the umbrella. There was no activity from the wildies. Normally they would roll for a few minutes as night set in, but not tonight.

Around midnight I had started to doze off. I was nice and snug on my waterproof ground sheet under the brolly, my pitch angled in such a way that the open front pointed directly at the pond, when I heard an odd sort of shuffling noise. One's hearing is heightened when your surroundings are deathly quiet. There was nothing else to distract me, my senses were locked onto that slinking, dragging sound. I tried not to move. I couldn't move! Were the ghostly monk's feet moving towards me? Then a bump against the side of the umbrella, and a rustle-sliding sound as if someone was dragging their hand across it. I quietly picked up a spare rod rest and waited in trepidation for someone, or something, to appear around the side.

A second slight bump, and that sliding noise again! Plucking up all of my courage I decided to meet the terror front on. Slowly, on hands and knees, I peeped around the side of the umbrella, fully expecting to encounter a dark hooded spectre.

I was confronted by a dark face with small, glazed eyes that glinted in the weak moonlight, followed by a loud "BAAAARR".

It was one of the farmer's black-faced sheep!

Laughing, and very relieved, I watched the equally scared sheep charge off into the now-thinning mist.

Still chuckling, I poured myself a cup of coffee and sat back to re-engage with my silver paper indicator. I'd only gotten it halfway drunk when the indicator twitched and rose about an inch. It dropped back as I gently grabbed the butt of the rod, then it slammed up against the butt ring. I lifted the rod and struck in one action. I was in another fight with a wildie of 4lb 4oz. A few minutes later it was in the net and I was happy to switch on my torch and see my prize. I unhooked it on a plastic sheet and wandered back to Mick for a photograph, and to relay my encounter with the ghost.

With the following dawn came the arrival of an extremely warm morning. The fishing went off and so we decided to give the pitches a rest and go for a wander. The farmer had a large number of pigs of all shapes and sizes, and he had told Mick earlier to keep well clear of the old male. He was huge, and I mean huge! A couple of days previous he had taken out a five-bar metal gate and a partition wall trying to get to the sows. Once he started rampaging nothing was going to stop him.

The newborn piglets were really cute but would insist on fighting all the time. We would verbally wager which piglet would come off worse when a dispute occurred, the result was often one losing half an ear or a chunk of a tail.

We fished Shobden right through the summer periods until the Autumn of 1971. It was always a great weekend, normally with lovely weather and successful fishing. I still don't know of many anglers who fish for wildies, maybe that's my ignorance, but I do recall a Mr. Chris Yates fishing for them on an estate lake in that great book *A Passion for Angling*.

As well as fishing at Shobden, we also revisited Llandrindod when we could organise a few days off work. So the summer of 1969 saw us once again travelling to central Wales in my trusty old van.

Leaving nothing to chance we planned everything, meticulously going over our tackle, the weather, and details of how we would sleep if we got exhausted. Night fishing in the 1960's and early 1970's could be tough going. A fold-up chair, umbrella and blanket were about as good as it got for comfort. So we decided that if one of us needed to crash out then we would use the back of the van.

I stole one of Mum's unused single mattresses from the spare room, which was just the right size to fit behind the front seats.

Before too long it became a permanent fixture and when not in use I covered it with a large piece of hardboard.

On arriving at the lake I parked up alongside a concrete wall. There was always plenty of room as there were only ever a couple of other anglers when we rocked up. Quickly we set up two pitches next to each other. The lake looked inviting with plenty of carp cruising backwards and forwards along the wall.

We had decided to fish mainly with freelined Yeoman spuds as they were partially boiled but still hard enough to cast a far distance without falling off the hook. They diced easily if a smaller bait was required, and they were cheap and available from most retail stores. Sometimes I would soak them in baked bean sauce, and if the carp didn't like them then Mick and I certainly did. The carp could also be caught on bread flake and juicy worms, especially around the lily pads.

Nested into the concrete wall was an old oak tree, the branches of which hung down and almost touched the lake's surface. This was one of my favourite pitches. Over the years the roots of the oak had also crept down the wall and into the lake. More than once I had dropped a bait down between the twisted roots and more than once was rewarded with a confident take from a resident carp. My first carp of 8lb 10oz was caught using this method and photographed by Mick. I am looking at that very photo as I write this paragraph.

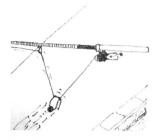

Fishing from the wall at night was enchanting, there was never complete darkness due to one or two streetlights around the lake perimeter. We would bait an area by the wall, and an hour or two later drop in a free-lined baited hook. Opening the bail arm we would use a silver paper indicator wrapped over the line, and with the aid of a small stone, lay it on the concrete slightly in tension. Then we would sit right next to the rods and wait. When a run started, the silver paper would rattle along the concrete and generally fall off when it slammed into the rod ring. The sound was magical. I can still hear it all these years on. And, if I am stalking carp and travelling light, I still use the same method. There is always a use for the silver paper from a block of chocolate, so I keep several neatly stored away in my tackle box. Plus it's a good excuse to eat chocolate right?

Our evening meals at Llandrindod Lake were always late affairs and we constantly forgot to eat. I lost track of the number of times a silver paper indicator would spring to life whilst Spam or sausages were sizzling away in the frying pan. That's when it's great to have a fishing buddy. When one of us was cooking the other could still be by the rods. If one of us needed the loo, or a wash, (yes, we did wash!), or to arrange the back of the van then the other would cover. But still, on more than one occasion, one could be playing a carp in one hand whilst balancing a hot pan in the other. We never wanted to put the pan on the ground in case it was pounced on by a passing dog or low-flying seagull. I guess we helped the local Co-Op improve their profit margins with the amount of food we purchased from them every time we fished the lake. We went there quite often over the years. At the ring of the till we were always greeted with a smile from the shop assistant as the greedy cash register gobbled up our hard-earned pounds.

There were never any people around after dark and, for the majority of the time, I felt very safe sitting quietly by my rods in the approaching darkness. I only ever had one worrying experience. Mick had gone for a walk and a visit to the toilet. Conditions had turned cold and a mist was drifting along the wall towards me. Also staggering towards me were two drunken young men. They started to mess around in our pitch and threatened to steal one of the rods. I picked up a landing net, my weapon of choice with which to defend our patch. Then out of the corner of my eye, I saw Mick heading back, completely unaware of what was going down. So I said to the two men, "You'd better watch out now, my boxing chum is about to arrive." They both followed my gaze and saw, to their alarm, a six-foot bloke coming out of the gloom. Mick's size was magnified by the shadows from the street lighting, and his duffle coat doubled the width of his shoulders. He had his head down and was striding along with purpose. He looked scary! Well, the two men took off in a flash, never to be seen again.

When Mick stepped up to the pitch he asked if he had missed anything. He meant with the fishing of course, and I replied that it had been quiet. I have never told him about the two men, I'm not sure why, so you will just have to trust me when I say it happened. Mick looked really scary that night, but the most terrifying thing about him is his farts. Oh yes, he's as much a champion trumpeter as he is a predator fisherman. We had many a contest as to who was the loudest or longest or could create the worst smell. The loser always had to make the next brew.

As darkness descended onto the lake, we would quietly bait up several areas close to the concrete wall. Knowing that sooner or later the carp would start patrolling the margins we would creep back an hour or so later and drop in a baited hook. Opening the bail arm and placing the silver paper indicator we would then lay the rods flat onto the concrete and quietly retire a few feet from the butt, waiting for an indicator to spring to life.

One late evening I was fishing under the oak tree whilst Mick was wandering around the lake. After a while, he returned and said to me, "John, come and have a look at this." We walked quietly back along the wall until we reached the corner pitch, close to where the rowing boats were tied up for the night. "Look at that tin and tell me if I'm going bonkers." There was a baked bean tin floating on the surface, open-end downwards. Now and then it would quickly disappear under the surface and then pop back up again. We watched fascinated, and lay on our stomachs to get a better view of what was occurring. We could just about see a pair of white lips approaching the tin from underneath. The mouth would suck and the can would then gently disappear under the surface.

"I'm sure that's a carp eating the beans from inside it," Mick retorted. The can spun, disappeared, and popped back up, only to disappear again a minute or two later.

"Well I never," I responded. We left the carp to its supper and returned to our van for a late meal of, you can guess, baked beans.

It was on a late July evening, with the half-moon rising and fishing under my favourite oak tree, that I lay listening to a much greater adventure than ours on the van's radio. It was 1969 and the first landing on the Moon's surface. The first moonwalk! I could say that just at that moment my silver paper indicator sprang into life, but that would be a lie. It is always said that people can remember what they were doing as the first moon landing took place. Well, I do. I was listening to the radio by the banks of a lake under a wise old oak tree. Same as it ever was!

During the warm summer days, the carp would cruise near or around the island in the centre of the lake. You could easily spot the carp when their dorsal fins broke the surface. We would change tactics on these days and fish floating crust, using the surface current to drift our baits, and additional free offerings, on a course to intercept the carp. The floating bread would always end up in the rowing boat corner, tight to the concrete wall. If luck was on our side a carp or two would be waiting to ambush the morsels. I had my first double-figure mirror carp by free-lining a piece of flake right under a moored rowboat. At the weekends visiting families would take to the row boats, armed with bread to feed the ducks and swans. It was before we knew better than to feed the birds bread. At five pm sharp all the boats would be called in and moored for the evening. We would wait for the families and boatman to leave and then, armed with a rod rigged for free lining, a landing net and a white loaf, we would quietly commence fishing under the boats. We were lucky if we caught more than one carp per row boat session though as the disturbance from a hooked carp always caused havoc. Often they would desperately try to shake the hook loose by crashing into the wall. The boats would violently rock in their wake as they shot under the bow. The fight was fast and furious. The rod would be bent double, the line scrapping along the bottom of the boats. There was no quarter given. Exciting or what?!

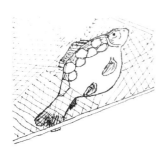

Mick caught the chubbiest mirror carp either of us had ever seen. It weighed 15lb 10oz and looked like it had eaten half of the loaf itself. We nicknamed it 'the football carp'. It makes me chuckle every time I look at the photo of it.

It was at Llandrindod that we first met angler, Mr Chris Yates. He was, of course, to become a legend in his own right. He was fishing the lake, I think for the first time, when he called for assistance in landing a big carp he had hooked. It was late in the evening. Mick was the first at the scene and duly netted the carp, which turned out to be Chris's first 20-pounder from the lake.

We visited the lake for three seasons and during that time fished many different parts of the lake. Mick had two more 15-pounders close to the children's boating pool, and we caught lots of carp from an area we named Green Banks. I had several good carp up to 14lb by float fishing bread and worms on the edge of a large patch of lilies.

It was around this time that battery-operated bite alarms started to appear in the tackle shops. I bought my first one from Greenway's Tackle Shop in Birmingham. My Dad helped Harold Greenway establish his first shop in Handsworth, and they became lifelong friends. Having purchased my Heron Bite Alarm I immediately regretted spending my money. It worked fine in dry weather, but, when wet or windy, it became a nightmare. It would either short out and go off randomly, or when it was windy the contacts would stick together and give false bite indications. If it got soaked it was necessary to dismantle it, dry it out, fit a new battery and then reassemble it, hoping that the very small retaining screw for the cover had not got lost. I think Mick was cannier than I on this subject. He was yet to be convinced about the construction and design of the Heron Alarms, and he was right.

With our carp catches now occasionally being published in the angling news, more anglers started to fish the lake. Like bees to the honey pot they came, and with them came more Heron Bite Alarms. When the Welsh rain and winds descended in all their glory we would laugh from the comfort of our umbrellas and blanket-covered bed chairs as we listened to the malfunctioning battery alarms, followed by the swearing of torch-holding anglers fumbling around in the dark. They'd try to reset their alarms more in hope than in confidence whilst the weather snatched at their clothes.

The very last straw that decided the fate of my Heron Alarm was on a late summer's evening. I hadn't slept for almost twenty-four hours and I needed to get my head down. As it was a warm evening, and very little wind had been predicted, I decided to use my alarm. I cast out towards the island and settled the rod in the rest. I clipped the line around the alarm's vertical contact and stretched out on my bed chair. It was not long before I fell asleep.

Well, Mick must have seen me snoozing and being in a mischievous mood, he crept along the water's shallows heading towards my rod. He very lightly, so as not to trigger the alarm, pulled off the slack line from my reel and quietly worked his way back to his pitch. After a short time, he tugged and tightened the line. The alarm contacts came together but the buzz failed to stir me in my slumber. So he did it again, using a longer pull. Now the buzzer registered in my sleeping brain! I shot up like a scalded cat and I struck hard at the non-existent carp. In my enthusiasm, I started to fall backwards. I scrambled to keep upright but failed, thus crashing into my umbrella which then collapsed onto my bed chair which then folded down flat. It sent me head over heels backwards. Mick was bursting with laughter, rocking backwards and forwards, the rotter! And so ended the short relationship between me and my Heron Bite Alarm. I saw one at a car boot last year and I was tempted until I noticed the small screw was missing. Plus the price tag was ridiculous!

Our specimen group, the SSSG, was gaining recognition in the Warwickshire area, and we decided it was time to invite new members. This is how Dennis Alcock became our latest recruit, and how he joined us at Llandrindod during one of our last sessions in 1973. The very first time he was night fishing he caught a lake record carp of 23lb 8oz. It can be such an unpredictable sport, fishing. It was his first carp from the lake and it was a corker!

He was using the first bolt rig Mick and I had ever seen. I believe it was long before it became the number one accepted method for catching carp, but Dennis's version was not the norm. He forgot to release his bail arm after casting in, and the carp just hooked itself. Luckily his backwinder was engaged, else more likely than not, he would have lost the lot.

The old van had started to give me suspension problems. One winter's chub fishing outing on the River Lugg with Mick, I was rattling along the rough track and it was making my steering erratic. The day had been hard going and very cold. It had been snowing when we arrived at the Lugg, but we had permission to drive over the field to the riverside, and we decided to still fish. That should not surprise anyone.

We only caught a couple of chub through the day and were thankful to get back into the van around mid-afternoon. As we returned across the field it became obvious we could not find our original route as the snow was a good three inches deeper. Our original tyre tracks had simply vanished. Steadily motoring across the field, my eyes focused on the exit gate, I suddenly rammed the van into a hidden bank and dropped into a deep snow-covered ditch. Now we were stuck in the middle of nowhere! Mick jumped out of the van and started foraging around, eventually finding some thick branches. With these, the car mats and an old blanket jammed under the wheels, I repeatedly reversed backwards and forward. Mick pushed while I steered. We finally cleared the ditch and, very relieved, trundled on towards the road-gate and finally onto the tarmac road.

The White Swan Club in 1969 had secured the fishing rights to a new lake in Worchestershire named Tern Mill in Osmington Village. The fish stock was controlled by the Severn/Trent Rivers Authority which used the lake as a holding and restocking facility. As spring arrived it didn't take long before we set out to investigate this new location. Tern Mill Lake was about six to eight acres, set in a small, lush valley and accessed along a typical primitive farmer's track. The track seemed endless but finally, we rounded a right-hand bend, and there was the lake, flat, calm, undisturbed and quiet. We were on our own on this beautiful lake which instantly became one of our favourite locations.

There was a decent head of carp in the lake, mostly mirrors, but it took quite some time and effort to get to grips with how to catch them. They were always very nervous and edgy especially during the day, even though they were under minimum pressure from anglers. However, we would fish the whole weekend and still have the lake to ourselves. Maybe it was the rutted track that put anglers off?

As it turned out, due to the thick blanket weed, we could only fish a limited number of pitches. My favourite was the reed beds at the top end of the lake where it was possible to watch the carp cruising through the reed stems. They'd occasionally stop to nose around in the silt and home in on one of our worm-baited hooks.

Mike however preferred the dam end of the lake and he fished with free-lined bread flake and floated crust. Over the next few seasons he developed his technique to such a degree that he caught almost every carp more than once from the lake. If you wish to read about his outstanding carp catches at Turn Mill it's all in Mick's book *Born to Fish*.

Our 'go-to' relaxing pitch was underneath a big old oak tree. This is where we would set up camp for the weekend. It had its own resident family of owls, (Mum, Dad and three littleuns), all of whom would sit on a branch and watch, heads swivelling intently with our every move.

We always endeavoured to keep the banks as undisturbed as possible, especially because leaving some cover helps prevent carp from spooking. Unfortunately though on this particular tree, there was one long thick branch which made casting in the dark very difficult. So one hot sunny morning, when the carp had retreated under the blanket weed, we decided the branch had to be shortened. I watched Mick attach a strong rope to the offending branch, the intention being to pull it back from the water's edge and cut off the offending piece. Well, it all got a bit silly very quickly. Mick decided he just had to have one swing on the rope before I cut it. Why? It's what big idiotic boys do on a sunny day when presented with a hanging rope and open water.

We'd had some rain the evening before, so in the shade of the tree, the ground was still slippery. Undeterred Mick grabbed the rope and shouted, "Watch Out John!" I stood back as Mick swung out on the rope, 'yahooing' as he went. He swung back under the tree and onto the bank, but in the excitement of the moment, he forgot the bank was wet.

His feet immediately slipped from under him. So 'Tarzan Brownie' is now sliding down the bank, feet trying to dig into the mud to slow the inevitable, still desperately hanging onto the spinning rope. With one final cry of alarm, as the bank became fresh air, he plunged into a good four feet of water and went under. He rose slowly from the depths, covered in thick weed, looking not unlike one of the sea creatures from John Herbert's film *The Mist*. I howled and howled with laughter.

Winter at Tern Mill was not just about carp fishing. We spent many an hour shaping out pitches and cutting back summer reed beds which seemed to spring up in the most unlikely places. During the winter season, worms were the most productive bait, but they were very frustrating to obtain. Mick started his own wormery which solved some of the problems, but on many occasions, I'd find a nice fat worm whilst digging out a bank to form a new pitch, and these worms were treated like gold until their final demise at the end of a sharp number 8 hook.

Although Mick and I never got tired of fishing together we also welcomed the opportunity to fish with the other members of the SSSG. Ken had moved down to Sopley in Hampshire, but still kept in touch. He persuaded us to fish for the Avon Barbel, and where better than on The Royalty Fishery waters? Getting a decent pitch in those days was difficult though. There'd be a queue of anglers who had arrived very early to grab the best pitches, and local anglers would reserve pitches for other locals. We eventually found a pitch just above and opposite the 'Pipes'. As we tackled up using our cane Avon carp rods, the weather started to change for the worse and it rained for the rest of the day.

We caught the odd chub, roach and a couple of barbel using maggots, but it soon became obvious that the barbel were preoccupied with the downstream pipes bank of the river. Late afternoon, after pints of maggots had been introduced into the river, the barbel would move in. We could only watch as fish after fish dragged the rod tips around, competing for the food source as we frustratedly looked on. It was a tough day and a tough lesson to take on board, travelling there and back in a weekend and being soaking wet for long periods. We chatted with Ken a few days later about our disappointing trip and Ken commented that we should try again for the barbel but at Sopley further upstream from Christchurch. It was a stretch hardly fished and as well as a shoal of barbel there was also some massive roach. He then sweetened the idea by showing us a photo of a fresh 25-pound salmon he had caught on maggots while fishing for the roach. He then added extra to the pot by telling us that he was also pestered by pike chasing his hooked roach.

I saw Mick's eyes light up and instinctively his reply was we needed to get down there again during the winter. After that we fished for pike at Sopley for three seasons from 1970 to

1972, always staying B&B at the New Queen Inn. I remember the breakfasts vividly. They had two big dogs, a Boxer and a Great Dane, and as soon as our 'full English' was being prepared, the Boxer would hide in wait in the kitchen. Then at the earliest opportunity, it would crawl towards our table, or should I say slide, legs splayed, tail acting as an oar. It would work its way under the tables until it came to one which was occupied, normally ours. It would wait expectantly for someone to give him a piece of bacon, or, if it was very lucky, half a sausage. If this didn't work it would huff and snort and bang its head on the underneath of the table, making the plates and cutlery rattle and jig about. This normally worked, and after devouring its treat it would then settle down on our feet. The Great Dane's favourite trick was to wait until the coast was clear in the kitchen, then it would charge in and grab whatever was on the work surface. One time it devoured half a pound of butter with one lick.

The stretch of the River Avon at Sopley was shallow and fast running. We started off trotting a bait through the weed beds, floats set so that the baits just occasionally touched the bottom. This produced many pike which would dart out from under the streamer weed, grab the bait and glide back under to devour their prize. Around lunchtime, whilst eating cheese and pickle sandwiches provided by the pub, we decided that the best method to locate the bigger pike would be to search out the back eddies and slacks and drop in a herring. This was our favourite bait and we dropped it into every likely spot we found. With the evening's shadows extending across the river the pike would move closer to the bank, and so improve our chances of a run.

One late afternoon on our second visit, Mick shouted over that he was desperate to go to the loo. It was likely due to the amount of alcohol we'd drank the previous evening. He dropped his float-fished dead herring right under the bank into small slack water by his feet, then quickly disappeared into a nearby bush, toilet paper in hand. From the depths of the bush, he shouted to me, just to make sure I was still on the opposite side, "John, old chap, keep an eye on my bung old bean." He sometimes went into posh English gentleman mode.

"Okay, don't you know", I replied in a similar voice. I sat down on the bank resting on my elbows and waited. It was not more than a couple of minutes when, out of the corner of my eye, I noticed Mick's float disappear under the river surface, then bob up again and gently start moving downstream. "Mick, I think you may have a run!"

"S*it", was the reply, followed by Mick crashing out of the bushes and stumbling to his rod, reel back winding as the float once again disappeared.

All I can say is that seeing Mick Brown's hairy white bum was not a sight I wish to revisit. He played and landed a lovely 11lb plus pristine pike, all the while trying desperately to pull up his pants.

Over the three seasons we caught some good pike. Most were in double figures, but we always had the feeling something better was eventually going to grab one of our herring dead baits, and sure enough Mick caught his first 20-pounder pike. At 20lb 8oz it was by far the biggest and best-looking pike we had ever seen. There were certainly some celebrations that night at the New Queens, and I was very happy for Mick's success. But, of course, I wished it had been my herring that the pike had homed in on.

All the pike we caught from Sopley were in excellent condition due to them having a constant quality food source and very little angling pressure. I did get a twenty-pounder from Sopley some years later, but that is a story for another time.

At the start of the seventies, I began dating my future wife Carol, and Mick also started dating Steph, his first wife, who very sadly died unexpectedly in 1988. Going out with the ladies at weekends reduced our fishing time and meant Mick and I were doing our 'own thing' a bit more. One mid-winter Sunday I had agreed to take a mutual friend from work named Gerry Harper to do some perch fishing. The lake we decided to fish was situated in one of Birmingham's many parks. This water had a reputation for holding some decent perch as well as a small head of double-figure carp. Circling the lake , which had unfortunately frozen over due to the recent bitterly cold winds, we came across a smaller lake with an overgrown island in the middle. Being more protected from the cold air there were expanses of clear water. Not wanting to disappoint Gerry I suggested we tried fishing for a few hours close to the island in one of the clear patches. I threw out a few handfuls of maggots, which were our bait for the session. Then, after waiting a few minutes, we cast out close to the island and sat back in our chairs waiting for the perch to show an interest. With a cup of hot coffee warming our hands, the cold snap didn't feel so bad. After about fifteen minutes I had my first perch of about 6 oz. Gerry quickly caught two more about the same size. After a quiet period, I hooked a bigger perch of 10 oz. It looked as if we were going to have a productive day.

But then out of the blue, we heard a cry for help from some distance away and towards the other larger lake. "Help! Help! My dog's fallen through the ice." An elderly gentleman was shouting and frantically waving his arms. He was pointing towards the frozen lake surface.

We could just see the head and front paws of a large dog, sloshing around in the icy water. It had run out onto the lake after being let off its lead and its weight had caused the thinner ice to crack. Being fond of dogs myself I ran towards the man, my waders badly hindering my progress. Arriving I could see that the dog was a St. Bernard. No wonder the ice had given way. The poor dog had now swum to the edge of the hole and was resting its head and paws on the top of the ice. "He won't be able to pull himself out," shouted the worried owner. The St. Bernard, on hearing its master voice, tried to again scramble out of the water, but its bulk and heavy wet coat of fur stopped any success. I shouted to Gerry to bring over the landing net, not sure how it was going to help but it seemed like a reasonable idea.

The owner was now really fretting, so I agreed I would try to reach

the dog by walking out into the icy water. I'm glad I had my waders on. I moved forward into the shallows and broke the ice with my hands and the landing net handle. I edged onwards carefully, feeling my way with my feet. The lake bottom seemed to be quite flat and the water was only just above knee level. Confident that I now had a workable plan, I forged forward, hammering and breaking the ice as I went. I got closer and closer to the dog, who was also getting more excited, its big brown eyes fixed on me the whole time. "Come on mate, you can do it," the dog seemed to be saying to me.

I was now almost within touching distance, only a few more feet to go. "Okay, this is it," I muttered through clenched teeth, and I took one more final step. "What the heck?" I'd stepped off the lake's shelf edge which was hidden under the ice and was now standing in four feet of murky, freezing water. It instantly gushed over the top of my waders, sending a chill down my legs and taking my breath away. "It's too late to go back now you idiot," I told myself, and taking a couple of deep breaths I grabbed the last sheet of ice between myself and the dog, and I heaved. It broke away with a loud crack.

The St. Bernard, seeing clear water in front of itself, started swimming with haste straight at me. Fearing it would doggy paddle me to death I tried to get out of its way. The dog narrowly missed me but the swirl as he passed made my feet slide out from under me. To stop myself from falling I grabbed its collar, and the dog pulled me into the safety of the lake shallows. Gerry quickly ran over and grabbing the landing net which I still had in my left hand, pulled me onto the grass bank. The dog meanwhile was enthusiastically jumping up at its master, and running around and around, shaking off the remains of the cold water.

I sat on the bank and emptied my waders, not believing what just happened. Then the elderly gent, as nice as you like, waved and simply said, "Thanks lads," before promptly walking off towards the park gates. The St. Bernard bounded after him. Gerry and I just looked at each other, and he shrugged and said, "You won't do that again in a hurry will you mate?" The trouble is, knowing me, I most likely would. A sucker or what?

Mick and I have helped rescue a fair number of different animals over the years. When we were at Slapton Ley, we saw a seabird in the distance slapping its winds in distress. It was difficult to identify the type of bird as it was completely black in colour. Rowing over we realised the bird was not black but covered head to tail in oil. Wrapping it up, after a quick struggle and a couple of pecks and scratches, we drove to the local RSPB hut. The little bird was still alive when we left. At least we had given it a chance.

We also rescued a family of Moorhens from the River Severn when it was running high and coloured. Mick, whilst fishing upstream from me, called out that a baby moorhen had just drifted past and was heading downstream. As it passed I was able to snatch it up in my landing net and I shouted to Mick that I had got it. Shortly afterwards, Mick alerted me again that there were more on the way. I scooped them up one by one as they came close and placed them side by side on the land where they all huddled together in a little hollow. We then gently picked them all up in a towel and carried them back upstream to reunite them with their mum who was fretting on the bank. I guess the rising water had washed the chicks out of the nest, and we just happened to be in the right place at the right time.

I helped the Sparey's son Anton drag a young calf out of a stream that ran through the lower meadow on the River Teme. The calf had tried to cross a very muddy part and got stuck, almost up to its belly. Using a stout rope around its shoulder, and with extra help from Anton's sister, we eventually pulled and pushed the calf onto dry land.

Whilst at Shobden Lakes on a very hot day, Mick accidentally hit a swallow whilst casting out. The bird, stunned, landed in the water. Mick quickly waded out and rescued it. Laying on his back in the sun Mick placed the bird on his chest to dry out its wings. It fully recovered about half an hour later and took off into the sky.

With more time being spent with our girlfriends it was normally only on a Sunday that we found the time to fish together. One particular Sunday we had arranged to meet on the river bank at Stanford Bridge. The Teme was running full but clear. Mick had arrived early and was already fishing for chub at his favourite pitch. I started to stalk the chub, walking upstream, when I came across Roger Pitt spinning for pike. I stopped a good ten yards away and watched him cast a No. 3 spinner across and under the tree line on the opposite bank. I was about to move towards him when I noticed a big pike resting by the reeds a few yards upstream. Quickly I laid my tackle down and crawled along the bank to get a better look. It was definitely a double!

Shuffling back from the bank and staying out of sight I walked up to Roger and told him about the pike. We quickly formulated a plan. Roger was to go down the bank, where on my instruction he would cast his spinner across the river under the trees and allow it to swing around with the current, finishing as close to the reeds as possible. My job was to lie back on the bank above the pike and tell Roger how close he was to getting his spinner to the striking zone. Crawling on hands and knees I looked over into the water and happily saw that the pike was still there. So I gave Roger the thumbs-up. He cast his Mepps spinner across and slightly downstream. It was the absolute perfect cast, the spinner hit the water and Roger clicked over the bale arm of his reel, the spinner stopped, and then started its rotating magic. The current pulled the spinner across the river, not only very close to the reeds but also directly in front of the pike's snout.

The pike hardly had to move, it just turned its head and engulfed the spinner. With a flaring of its gills and a shake of its head, the fish turned downstream. I jumped up and shouted, "Roger! Strike, it's got it," but Roger already knew. His Alcocks Carp rod had lunged over as the pike made the first run for freedom. I watched as the fish twisted and turned, bending Roger's rod into a lovely curve as it surged and charged for the safety of the tree line. The pike slowly came to the net and we carried it to the top of the bank after carefully unhooking the spinner. It was weighed at exactly 12lb. What a result! When flicking through my fishing albums I come across the photo I took at the time. Army logistics could not have done a better job than Roger and I on that occasion.

It was around this time that I finally had to sell my trusty old van. My replacement was an Austin Healey Sprite, but before long it developed an occasional habit of jumping out of third gear. Mick and Steph were now buying a house in Shirley, Solihull and he offered me the use of his garage. He also agreed to help sort out the gearbox problem. With both of us being mechanical engineers we ended up not only sorting the gearbox but also fitting a new camshaft, reskimming the engine block and fitting a new manifold system complete with a straight-through exhaust. Now the souped-up Sprite got a move on and it was always a thrilling little car to drive.

In 1973 I was offered an overseas three-year contract in New Zealand working for Lucas Industries installing new production lines. Also in September 1973, I married my lifelong partner, Carol. After a short honeymoon, we were heading to Heathrow, preparing to board the Qantas plane for our thirty-two-hour flight to Auckland. It was tough leaving family and friends, and especially my buddy Mick. I told myself it would only be for three years. However, it ended up being a five-year contract, and an experience I will never forget or regret going. My Dad sold the Sprite and sent me the proceeds which helped us with settling in costs.

During the late seventies, Mick moved from Brum to Market Deeping with his two young children. It was a tough time for Mick as Lucas's was gradually folding up. He had to find new employment to support his family. His passion for predator fishing finally saw him, in the '90s, taking the plunge to become a professional angler, specialising in the predator species. The rest is angling history. Mick became one of the best of his trade and has earned a highly respected place in the angling oracles. For me, I have been there right from the beginning and would not change any of our adventures either good or bad.

So now I have come to the end of the first ten years of our friendship. Little did I know at the time that it would be another fifteen years before we would get the opportunity to meet up and resume our fishing adventures. But when we did meet it was just like old times. We were older and wiser, but relaxed and glad to be back in each other's company. As I think about these later years I get the feeling another book is on the cards. There are plenty more memories already flooding my head.

THE END...maybe

ABOUT THE AUTHOR

John Anscombe

John Anscombe, born in Birmingham in 1947, is the youngest of three brothers. His lifelong passion for fishing was sparked at the age of 6 when his father took him fishing to the Sutton Coldfield boating lake. Over 70 years later, that passion remains as strong as ever.

Beginning his career as an indented engineering apprentice, John honed his skills to become a skilled toolmaker and eventually transitioned into a role as a tool design draughtsman. Later in his career, he ascended to the position of design and development manager, specializing in distribution logistics.

Alongside his love for fishing, John enjoys rugby, badminton, and gardening. Throughout his life, he has been supported and guided by his loving wife Carol, with whom he has shared 50 years of marriage.

John continues to indulge in his passion for fishing whenever the opportunity arises, finding solace and joy in the timeless pursuit of reeling in the day's catch.

Printed in Great Britain
by Amazon